CRUNCH POINTS FO

Julia Cole is a trained couple co............., ..,
therapist and counselling supervisor with Relate; she is
also Press Officer for National Relate. In addition, she is
the Problem Page editor for *Essentials* magazine, and a
freelance writer and broadcaster on relationship issues.
She is married to Peter, and has two children, Adam and
Hannah.

Overcoming Common Problems Series

For a full list of titles please contact
Sheldon Press, Marylebone Road, London NW1 4DU

The Assertiveness Workbook
A plan for busy women
JOANNA GUTMANN

Beating the Comfort Trap
DR WINDY DRYDEN AND JACK
GORDON

Birth Over Thirty Five
SHEILA KITZINGER

Body Language
How to read others' thoughts by their
gestures
ALLAN PEASE

Body Language in Relationships
DAVID COHEN

Calm Down
How to cope with frustration and anger
DR PAUL HAUCK

Cancer – A Family Affair
NEVILLE SHONE

The Candida Diet Book
KAREN BRODY

Caring for Your Elderly Parent
JULIA BURTON-JONES

Comfort for Depression
JANET HORWOOD

Coping Successfully with Hayfever
DR ROBERT YOUNGSON

Coping Successfully with Migraine
SUE DYSON

Coping Successfully with Pain
NEVILLE SHONE

Coping Successfully with PMS
KAREN EVENNETT

Coping Successfully with Panic Attacks
SHIRLEY TRICKETT

**Coping Successfully with Prostate
Problems**
ROSY REYNOLDS

**Coping Successfully with Your
Hyperactive Child**
DR PAUL CARSON

**Coping Successfully with Your Irritable
Bowel**
ROSEMARY NICOL

**Coping Successfully with Your Second
Child**
FIONA MARSHALL

Coping with Anxiety and Depression
SHIRLEY TRICKETT

Coping with Blushing
DR ROBERT EDELMANN

Coping with Breast Cancer
DR EADIE HEYDERMAN

Coping with Bronchitis and Emphysema
DR TOM SMITH

Coping with Candida
SHIRLEY TRICKETT

Coping with Chronic Fatigue
TRUDIE CHALDER

Coping with Crushes
ANITA NAIK

Coping with Cystitis
CAROLINE CLAYTON

Coping with Depression and Elation
DR PATRICK McKEON

Coping with Eczema
DR ROBERT YOUNGSON

Coping with Endometriosis
JO MEARS

Coping with Psoriasis
PROFESSOR RONALD MARKS

Coping with Schizophrenia
DR STEVEN JONES AND DR FRANK
TALLIS

Coping with Stomach Ulcers
DR TOM SMITH

Coping with Thyroid Problems
DR JOAN GOMEZ

Coping with Thrush
CAROLINE CLAYTON

Coping with Your Cervical Smear
KAREN EVENNETT

Crunch Points for Couples
JULIA COLE

Curing Arthritis Exercise Book
MARGARET HILLS AND JANET
HORWOOD

Overcoming Common Problems Series

Overcoming Common Problems Series

Living with Asthma
DR ROBERT YOUNGSON

Living with Diabetes
DR JOAN GOMEZ

Living with Grief
DR TONY LAKE

Living with High Blood Pressure
DR TOM SMITH

Making the Most of Yourself
GILL FOX AND SHEILA DAINOW

Menopause
RAEWYN MACKENZIE

Migraine Diet Book, The
SUE DYSON

Motor Neurone Disease – A Family Affair
DR DAVID OLIVER

The Nervous Person's Companion
DR KENNETH HAMBLY

Out of Work – A Family Affair
ANNE LOVELL

Overcoming Anger
DR WINDY DRYDEN

Overcoming Guilt
DR WINDY DRYDEN

Overcoming Stress
DR VERNON COLEMAN

The Parkinson's Disease Handbook
DR RICHARD GODWIN-AUSTEN

The PMS Diet Book
KAREN EVENNETT

Serious Mental Illness – A Family Affair
GWEN HOWE

Sleep Like a Dream – The Drug-Free Way
ROSEMARY NICOL

Subfertility Handbook, The
VIRGINIA IRONSIDE AND SARAH
BIGGS

Talking About Anorexia
How to cope with life without starving
MAROUSHKA MONRO

Ten Steps to Positive Living
DR WINDY DRYDEN

Think Your Way to Happiness
DR WINDY DRYDEN AND JACK
GORDON

**Understanding Obsessions and
Compulsions**
A self-help manual
DR FRANK TALLIS

Understanding Your Personality
Myers-Briggs and more
PATRICIA HEDGES

A Weight Off Your Mind
How to stop worrying about your body size
SUE DYSON

When your Child Comes Out
ANNE LOVELL

Overcoming Common Problems

CRUNCH POINTS FOR COUPLES

Julia Cole

First published in 1997 by
Sheldon Press, SPCK, Marylebone Road, London NW1 4DU

British Library Cataloguing-in-Publication Data
A catalogue record for this book is available from the British Library

ISBN 0-85969-743-6

Photoset by Deltatype Ltd, Birkenhead, Merseyside
Printed in Great Britain by Biddles Ltd, Guildford

Contents

Dedication

For Peter, Adam and Hannah –
and
for all those couples I have been privileged to counsel
at Relate during the last ten years

Introduction

This book is about change. Change can be exciting, exhilarating and challenging, but it can also be frightening, stressful and unexpected. Change can seem difficult enough to deal with when you are on your own, but if you are part of a couple, it can seem even more complex. Not only do you have to sort out your own feelings about the change you are facing, but you also have to take into account the feelings and behaviour of your partner. It can seem like a complicated dance in which you cannot always follow the beat, and where neither one of you is sure of the steps!

Many of the couples I have seen in counselling have told me about the problems that change has presented in their relationship. Sometimes these changes have been planned for, and perceived as positive – like having a first child, for instance. Other couples have described the devastating effects of dealing with change that they hoped they would never have to cope with – perhaps illness, or the aftermath of an affair. I have often been asked if couples take their relationships less seriously today than they did 30 or 40 years ago. I can honestly say I have never met a couple (especially those who get married) who told me they didn't choose to be together, or saw themselves as anything other than destined for a lifetime together. However, what most couples *do* tell me is that they were unprepared for the changes that they encountered as their relationship progressed. They found that these changes often prevented them from sharing feelings and thoughts, and sometimes prevented them from taking action to solve the difficulties they were presented with. They felt as if they had been 'frozen' by the change, and didn't know how to deal with the fall-out from the effects of the change they were facing.

'Crunch points'

As I met more and more couples, it seemed clear to me that there were some types of change that were by far the hardest to deal with. I see these as 'crunch points' – times when couples find themselves up against tough decisions and feelings. As you read this book, you will find chapters on these especially difficult times. These include:

- How relationships grow.
- Coping with becoming parents.

1

- The impact of money concerns in relationships.
- Sexual worries for you and your partner.
- Loss of trust in your relationship – especially as a result of an affair.
- Dealing with change you cannot control, e.g. illness or death.
- Realizing your partnership has broken down.

Each chapter describes the common feelings surrounding these events, and ways to understand and deal with them. Many of the couples I see in counselling have told me that it has been helpful to understand that they were not alone in feeling very knocked by these crunch points. As I worked with these couples, we discovered that different types of change were accompanied by different types of feelings. Sometimes the feelings resulting from particular changes had a pattern, but other changes were accompanied by emotions that seemed random.

Responding to change

Listening to couples showed me that there were helpful and unhelpful responses to crunch points, and that these different responses from each partner could make the difference between the relationship surviving and adapting, or breaking down. Helpful responses (Chapter 1) enable couples to look forward in their relationships, and to make shared adjustments that help to build up the relationship. I am not suggesting that responding openly and honestly in a difficult situation is easy; it can often be painful and demanding to stick to accepting personal responsibilities, and acknowledging the need for change. It is much easier to blame someone else, or to try to push the whole difficult problem under the carpet. These unhelpful responses can initially feel simpler, but in the long term can act like a cancer in a relationship. Although apparently out of sight, unhelpful responses can eat away at a couple's respect for one another, or sense of trust, and eventually cause the relationship to die.

How change is really a circle

Most change is circular. We tend to imagine that life is lived in a straight line, and that we travel forward from new experience to new experience, without a backward glance. In reality, most couples I see describe the change they are going through as having distinct steps of phases. These phases are often similar, despite the type of problem they are dealing with, and are more fully described in Chapter 1.

Sometimes each phase of change is short, but at other times it is longer. Or a couple may get 'stuck' at a certain step, and then race through the next step.

A good image of change might be to see yourself and your partner as sitting in a wheel. As the wheel rolls along the road, you are moving forward, but also going round and round in the wheel. How you experience the road will depend upon how you feel about the wheel you are in together. Learning how to cope with change can give you a much more comfortable ride, and help both of you to feel closer to one another. This book may also help you to recognize stress points before you meet them.

How relationships develop

Many people I have counselled see relationships as static: they believe that how they were when they first met is how they should be for the rest of the relationship. It is as if they think they should still wear a Babygro at 35! Some people solve this need to change 'clothes' by changing partners. They enter a new stage of development, and cast off their old partner for a new one. Of course, some partners do grow apart, and find that their interests or shared goals become so divergent that they can no longer make them fit each other. Most relationships, though, go through different stages of development, and understanding these can help you to cope with the ups and downs of a growing relationship. Chapter 2 will help you identify the different stages that your relationship might pass through, and how to utilize skills to help you deal with each stage.

More and more couples are worried about their relationships, and the divorce rate is rising in the UK. There are lots of different reasons for this, and many of them are probably quite complex. One thing is certain, though – we have certainly moved a long way from the familiar pattern of the 'wife at home and dad at work'. Today when we talk about 'families' or 'relationships' we are just as likely to mean a single parent, a family with step-children, an unmarried couple living together, and many other permutations. Having counselled many different types of couple relationships over the years, I know that understanding the nature of relationships, and the way in which they cope with change, is crucial for a healthy, loving relationship. This book is designed to help you understand, and then put into action, ways to keep your relationship alive.

1

The Cycle of Change

All relationships change, and the evidence of this change is all around us. If you take a trip to your local shopping centre, you will see young lovers gazing into each other's eyes, new parents pushing prams, and older people strolling along together. However, accepting that *we ourselves* change, both as individuals and as part of a couple, can seem more difficult to get to grips with. Many couples feel that if the nature of their relationship changes at all, then this is something that somehow just happens, rather than something that they may decide or plan for.

Some couples fear change, and see any potential for taking a different direction in their relationship as threatening, something to be avoided. Others don't realize the full impact of a change in lifestyle until they are in the middle of coping with the feelings that have come from the change – whether it be a house move, or choice of job. Once you have both made a commitment to each other, it may seem as if this first commitment will see you through – like the foundations beneath a house. If a house doesn't have reasonable foundations, then it is likely to collapse. But the foundations of relationships (unlike houses) need constant maintenance if they are to remain strong and secure. For, as with houses, if the foundations crumble, then a crisis will easily undermine the whole structure.

In terms of these foundations, there are some 'basics' that couples everywhere share. For example, most people say they need to be able to trust their partner; they may also say they need to share common goals in life – whether it is bringing up children, or enjoying leisure-time together. Sometimes, couples talk about 'being there for each other' – suggesting a desire to know there will be support when times are tough, or shared pleasure during the good times. However, the basics of a shared relationship will also reflect the uniqueness of that relationship. You may be able to think of highly individual 'basics' in your own relationship – or relationships you have had in the past.

As a couple counsellor, I know that many couples do talk to each other about their expectations and hopes when they are first building their relationships. It can be a very exciting time, as each partner discovers what the other one thinks and feels, and a strong sense of what they each expect from this partnership is gradually formed. Most people would call this 'falling in love'. If you think about the term 'falling in love', it suggests taking a dive, a risk, into something unknown and strange. We seem to accept this at the start of a relationship, perhaps because it may still be possible to pull out if we find we have made a misjudgement in our choice of partner. However, as a relationship deepens, it can seem harder to take risks – perhaps to talk about difficult issues, for example. It is as if once an investment has been made, couples may pull back a little, and live on the 'interest' they have 'saved' in their 'relationship bank'. This is a natural pattern, but can cause problems if couples attempt to live on these 'savings' for the rest of the relationship. To stretch the banking image even further, it is as if they go on depending on the support of a diminishing account. However, relationships need investments, of time and effort, if they are to survive over a long period.

This way of looking at relationships shows that there are problems with hanging your *whole* future relationship on the first set of shared commitments you make. Sticking rigidly to them takes no account of changes that you may meet as you go through life together. For example, you may decide that travel is a vital component of your life together, and happily spend the early years of your life together exploring the countryside or taking holidays abroad. If you stuck to this commitment as time progressed, despite the baby screaming on every journey, or insisted on an expensive foreign holiday although you had lost your job, your relationship would soon start to feel under severe stress. Relationships depend upon negotiation and adjustment to help them work successfully. With flexibility your relationship can survive change, rather than snap beneath the weight of it.

Case history
Martin and Susan had been married for six years. They had a son of 18 months and a daughter aged 3. They had met through a shared interest in football, and Susan spent many of their first dates at their local club, cheering Martin on. Things were fine – until their daughter was born. Susan gave up going to games during pregnancy, but Martin continued to spend many weekends at the club. At first, Susan didn't mind too much as she was busy preparing for the baby. But when their second baby, a son, arrived, Susan began to feel increasingly isolated. Martin had also begun to try to persuade her to go with him on football trips, and to leave the children with friends. She felt he didn't understand her need for practical support with two small children, while Martin felt she was no longer interested in the sport that had brought them together – or in him. Both became resentful, and felt that the other should understand without having their needs spelt out to their partner.

Eventually, Susan became very angry with Martin as he prepared to leave for the club one Saturday morning. They had a terrible row, and Martin drove off in the car. While they were apart, both felt miserable at the unhappiness they had caused each other. When he came back, they decided they had to tackle the root of the problem. Martin explained he had often felt left out since the children were born and, although he loved them, he sometimes missed just being a couple. He realized he had used the club as a way of avoiding tackling his emotions, partly because he felt guilty at feeling jealous of his own children. Susan told Martin that she had changed, and was less interested in football now, but wanted to support him. However, she also wanted help with the children, and more time with Martin and the children as a family unit. They agreed that Martin would spend less time at the club, and help Susan around the house. Susan suggested that she occasionally went along to the club to cheer Martin on. They also tried to make more time for each other, and grew to value time alone to talk.

Martin and Susan took a vital step in understanding their unhappiness by being willing to look at, and discuss, the root of their problems. They were also able to decide to make changes that were suitable to their needs at the time. These needs are likely to change in the future, but they now know they can negotiate successfully.

For you to try – what are your *basics*?

- What do you think are the 'basics' in your relationship?
- Make a list of those things that you believe are most important to the foundations of your relationship. Include anything you know it would be very difficult to do without. You might choose 'faithfulness' or 'a cuddle when I feel low'. There are no right or wrong answers, just those things that are right for you.
- Now try to cast your mind back to the start of your relationship. Would your answers have differed then?
- Have you changed anything fundamentally, or added something important? If there have been significant changes, reflect on how you handled the change. You can either do this exercise on your own or with your partner. Alternatively, you could draw up separate lists and then share the results. You may find that you agree on some areas, but not on others. Use the lists to help you think about the way your relationship has developed.

The circle of change

Coping with life changes can often seem like an uphill path, especially if you are enmeshed in struggling with a big change in your life, like separation or money worries. It's common to feel 'if I can just get through this next bit, I can move on to the next part of my life'. But change is more like a rolling circle. A good way of explaining this might be to see dealing with change as being like the seasons. Each year the same things happen – daffodils appear, green leaves grow, and the sun returns. As the seasons pass, colder weather returns, the leaves fall, and winter comes. However, each year is slightly different to the year that went before. Spring might come early, or we might have a cold or warm summer.

Change that you experience in your life will be like this pattern. The way that you react to present or future change will be influenced by how you've handled change in the past. You may even notice that you tend to respond in a certain way – perhaps by keeping your head down and saying little, or telling everybody what you feel. In other words, you may have noticed that the same things often happen to you as you approach change, although they may not be played out in exactly the same way. So although the actual event that has caused the change is different, the manner in which you approach it can be similar. The way in which you deal with change will also fit into a larger cycle as the change you are coping with moves through several stages of development. You may not always notice these stages as they happen to you, but most life changes pass through the following phases:

Stage 1

At first, you have little idea that change is coming, or is needed. Sometimes, one partner feels something needs to be different before the other does, and this can cause tension. Arguments that arise at this stage can often seem very frustrating, with one partner blaming the other for deliberately not understanding their concerns. The partner who sees no need to take action is unlikely to be deliberate in their misunderstanding, but perhaps they have not reached the same stage as their partner.

Stage 2

This stage is followed by either a slow awareness of the need for change, or a sudden need to cope with a crisis. Change may be forced upon a couple by outside circumstances – such as having a baby, or trouble paying the mortgage. It can also feel like an inner need that gradually wells up inside, such as feeling you are being taken for granted. You may find you have trouble putting into words exactly what you would like to be different, but are very well aware of the need to make changes in your relationship. At this stage, it may take some time to make sense of your thoughts and emotions, but eventually you are likely to decide to take action.

Stage 3

This is probably the stage at which most couples notice the full effects of a change in their relationship. It is possible to skate over stages 1 and 2, sometimes with little disturbance, but the action stage is nearly always a difficult time. *Deciding* to do something differently, and actually *attempting* it, can be worlds apart. What seemed workable on paper, or in your mind, may hit unseen snags once you implement change. You may have jointly decided that it is right to tackle your teenage son on the state of his bedroom, but still be unprepared for the hard work of maintaining a united front while he argues with you both. At this point, disagreements over change may be heated, or communication may be strained, as you both try to cope with individual feelings about the decision you have taken.

Stage 4

Now that you have worked through some of the stages of the circle, and tried out some of the changes you want, this stage may feel like a lull. If the change has worked well, you will gradually build on what you have already achieved – sometimes renegotiating any problem areas. If you are dissatisfied, then you might use this time to draw breath, and return to stage 2 for a while, as you reassess why you are not completely satisfied. If one partner is more satisfied than the other, you may feel as if you are repeatedly trying to explain to each other what you feel. Your partner may want to hang on to what seems to work for them, leaving you uncertain and guilty at wanting further changes.

Stage 5

Change that has been handled well will lead to this stage. You will feel more secure, and less anxious about facing the future. You may notice an increased ability to talk to your partner, and an improved sense of closeness. This will also mean that as more change is tackled, you will be able to use your experiences to work through the earlier stages more successfully. If there have been problems, you are likely to find yourself moving backwards around the circle, or even re-entering at stage 1.

The reason I describe this cycle as a rolling circle is because most of us are usually at one of these different stages throughout our lives – whether we are single or in a partnership. We begin to learn about change from the moment of birth. Sometimes, though, we learn ways of coping with change that cause difficulties with our partners or other members of the family.

Case history

Pauline and Stewart had lived together for two years when Stewart lost his job. The firm he worked for went into liquidation, and he was left wondering if he would ever find a job again. Pauline worked full time as a travel agent, and was very worried about Stewart's unemployment, although she kept this worry to herself. She didn't think they could survive on the money they had coming in.

Stewart came from a family where to be without money was to be seen as a failure, and perhaps even labelled as lazy. He could dimly remember his father having money troubles when he was a child. Stewart's mother had kept a stony silence on the subject, and it had never been discussed, although Stewart knew that cash was in short supply for at least two years during his childhood. Although Stewart's job loss was not his responsibility, he felt guilty and miserable. Pauline tried to talk to him, but he behaved just as his family had done, and shared very little with Pauline. He justified this to himself as saving Pauline from unnecessary worry, but it made Pauline feel extremely insecure.

As the months went by, with no job on the horizon, Pauline and Stewart grew further and further apart. Eventually, Pauline told Stewart she couldn't live with him any longer, and left to live alone. Stewart felt awful, and told himself that his family's attitude had been true – becoming poorer did cause people to see you as a failure. He felt certain that Pauline had left because she saw him as worthless now that he was out of work. Stewart eventually attended counselling sessions at his local doctor's surgery, where he was helped to reaize that his relationship with Pauline had truly finished. This was not because of his job loss, but because it had been so hard for him to share any of his worries with Pauline. Although he could not repair his partnership with Pauline, he understood that his family's method of dealing with difficult change was likely to cause problems in future relationships. He could see that he needed to be more open about his thoughts and feelings if other partnerships were to be successful.

How couples respond to change

When the circle of change is worked through successfully it can enhance and strengthen a relationship. However, as Pauline and Stewart's case history illustrates, it can be pulled off course by unhelpful responses from both partners. There are several common ways in which couples deal with change. Use the descriptions below to see how you think you may deal with change (planned or not); I have compared helpful and unhelpful approaches, although most couples use a mixture of these throughout their relationship. Every relationship can tolerate some unhelpful responses, but if a couple begin to feel weighed down by their negative approach to change, they may find that their relationship becomes stagnated and constricting.

Unhelpful responses

1 Denial

This response can be shared by both people in a relationship, or acted out by just one member. It commonly occurs when change becomes fairly obvious to both, but neither feels able to tackle the issues involved. In a sense, the couple 'pretend' nothing is wrong, and thus that no change is needed, even though it may seem obvious to others. For instance, a couple may ignore the rising amount of debt on their credit card, hoping that 'something will happen' to prevent them having to pay back a large amount of money. If just one person in the partnership denies the need for change, it not only causes frustration, but it may feel as if both partners are pulling in opposite directions. Sometimes, denying the importance of a difficult situation can mask very painful emotions that the couple are afraid to tackle, and this type of response is common in relationships where a split seems imminent. None of this may be consciously thought through, but it can happen as a subconscious reaction.

2 Avoidance

In this response to changing circumstances, a couple may be aware of a problem that needs addressing. They may even attempt to take action, but it will feel half-hearted and will fail to deal with the difficulty successfully. The couple may find that the problem dies away for a short while, only to resurface later. Sometimes the same difficulty keeps returning, but in a slightly different form, because it has not been properly dealt with.

Case history

For several months after their marriage, Andrew and Jan argued over Andrew's weekly night out with his mates. Eventually, Jan grew exhausted with rowing, and suppressed her irritation. The rows stopped, until Jan's friends invited her along for a regular girls' night out. At this point, Andrew felt annoyed with Jan, and accused her of losing interest in him. Neither of them had sorted out the initial problem about how much time they should spend together, and how much time apart, so the difficulty came back to haunt them.

3 Blaming

To blame, or feel blamed, is perhaps the most hurtful response to the prospect of change. One partner may become aware of change on the horizon, and respond by feeling threatened and anxious. Instead of enlisting their partner's help to cope, they blame their partner for not protecting them from the change ahead. They may even hold their partner to be totally responsible for the change, and demand that they alter their behaviour to prevent the change from affecting them in any way.

Case history

Karen felt this way when her boyfriend, Mike, told her he felt unsure about their relationship, and wanted a temporary break to reassess his feelings for her. Karen had also felt there was something wrong in their relationship, but had been afraid to talk to Mike about her worries. She felt that if she admitted any of her emotion, it would immediately spell the end of the two of them. When Mike told her of his decision, Karen told him angrily that this break proved he was uncommitted to the relationship. She told him she had seen problems coming, but Mike's response proved it was all his fault because he had failed to work at the relationship as he should have done. Mike felt pushed out by Karen, and even more uncertain about their future. Karen blamed Mike for forcing change upon them both, when in reality she knew that there were faults on both sides.

A variation on blaming can occur. Instead of blaming each other for creating, or not solving, a difficulty, the couple cast about for someone (or something) to blame for their inability to cope with change. It is as if the couple 'close ranks' to keep the worry about change at arm's length, which also avoids facing their shared problem.

Case history
Simon and Carol had been unhappy in their marriage for some months. They argued constantly, and felt unable to resolve their differences. Carol couldn't work out why this was happening, although she was aware that she had felt differently about herself, and the marriage, since she had reached 40. Some while later, she discovered that Simon was having an affair. She was very angry, but not with Simon. She went to the other woman's house, and told her to leave Simon alone. She saw Simon as the victim of a 'predatory woman', someone who was destroying their relationship. Carol lost sight of her previous uncomfortable feelings about herself and Simon, and blamed all their troubles on the other woman. She was afraid to confront the deeper issues that were connected to her own feelings and emotions about how she and Simon related.

It will be clear from the description of these unhelpful responses to change that most couples do not set out to deny or avoid change. These responses normally come from learnt behaviour from the past, or hide deep feelings of hurt and mistrust that many people find it hard to admit to. This fear of personal vulnerability that can contribute to blaming behaviour can also be unseen by the couple until a specific event brings the blaming to light.

Helpful responses

1 Acknowledgement of the need for change

Of all the responses that change requires of a couple, this is the most crucial. Couples who are able to accept the idea of change as an integral part of their union will be better equipped to meet the challenge of change when it comes along. It is possible to see a relationship as a tapestry in which the picture is never finished, and constantly changing. It may seem that particular colours are dominant at certain times, or that the tapestry may need to be unpicked to sew a particular section differently. There may be threads that are laid down, only to be picked up again later. A tapestry woven in this way would be exciting to look at, and never boring to sew! It is these qualities, of excitement, pleasure and fulfilment, that can be gained from understanding that change is inevitable, rather than an enemy to be fought off.

2 Acceptance of your personal role

At first sight, 'acceptance' may seem to imply that you should blindly take on whatever fate throws at you; however, this is not what is being said. Neither is it being suggested that you should behave in a self-deprecating way – i.e. accepting responsibility for the need to change in a martyrish way.

Acceptance can mean a willingness to take personal responsibility for your part in the change ahead. It may seem, at first sight, as if your role is likely to be small. You may even feel that the concern, whatever it is, has nothing to do with you. However, if you demonstrate acceptance, then you will begin to ask more effectively what you can do to make a difference to any situation. This approach will also prevent your own defences from rising so high that you shut your partner out. Rather than the closed, excluding, behaviour of denial and avoidance, you can open up tough situations so that they lose the power to hurt.

Case history

Alice and Sam found this approach useful when Alice had to have an operation on her breast. Alice felt terrified by this because her mother had died of breast cancer. She found it hard to tell Sam her fears, and at first Sam felt he could do little to help Alice. As the date for the operation approached, Alice became increasingly silent; Sam reacted by feeling hurt. He felt that Alice did not trust him, and then found himself withdrawing, feeling hurt that Alice valued him so little.

The night before Alice was to go into hospital, Sam found her weeping in their bedroom. He asked her to tell him how she was feeling, but she turned away. Sam felt a wave of frustration wash over him, and nearly left the room. However, he couldn't bear to see Alice so unhappy, so sat down by her, gently taking her hand in his. He said nothing, and gradually Alice turned towards him and allowed herself to be held.

As the evening wore on, Alice was able to explain her very real anxiety. Both felt strengthened by this experience, and they had a real sense of facing the operation together. Sam accepted he had a role to play, even though it had not seemed obvious what this should be. Alice was helped to share her fears, although this was not easy for her.

3 Reassessment of the situation

Reassessment can seem the last thing you want to do if a life change appears wholly negative. The desire to allow the change to wash over you, while possibly blaming others, or avoiding facing a situation, can seem by far the easiest solution.

Case history

Jenny felt like this when she knew that her youngest child was about to leave home, her other children having already left. Jenny had been married only seven years when she was widowed, and had taken great comfort from her three children. Friends and relatives admired her selfless attitude towards her children. In many ways, her children had been her whole life, and she had put off thinking about the time when she would be on her own. Jenny's two sons and daughter were a credit to her, and she felt proud of their families and careers. But now her son, Nick, was about to begin work for a company some distance away, and she felt deserted. Life seemed to have lost all its colour, and she became depressed. Jenny could not see how life could be worth living once she was truly alone in her once busy house.

It was then that Jenny's daughter, Viv, visited her. She asked her mother about her depressed feelings, and Jenny told her tearfully about her dread of living alone. Viv asked her mother to do a surprising thing – she asked her to think of all the things she could do once Nick left. Jenny was furious with Viv, and felt even more hurt that her daughter could be so tactless. Yet over the next few days, Jenny found Viv's question playing on her mind, and new ideas began to enter her thoughts. She realized she would be able to eat what she really wanted to eat, instead of always catering to Nick's tastes. She also decided she might take up her friends' offer of a shared holiday, without having the worry as to whether Nick could manage alone. Slowly, Jenny reassessed her feelings, and was able to see Nick's move as a door opening on to new possibilities, alongside her sadness at his leaving.

Jenny didn't find it easy to reassess her feelings, but reassessment can offer the chance to 'reframe' a difficult situation. It is similar to taking an old picture – perhaps one you saw as worthless – and then cleaning and reframing it. When you do this, colours can seem brighter, and you may even notice new things you hadn't seen before. Sometimes an art expert may tell you that the picture you once saw as ugly is actually worth something. In Jenny's case, Viv acted like the art expert by helping Jenny to see new value in what seemed a worthless situation.

4 Looking at the choices available

You may think that this category is obvious, and that people always examine all the choices open to them when the need for change becomes clear. However, many couples do not look at the range of choices open to them. Many people plump for the first option they think of, and then find themselves hemmed in by further complications. These can be avoided by considering all the paths you might follow. Taking the first option can be the result of tiredness, perhaps because of worrying about the difficulty over a long period. It is not unlike buying the first thing you can lay your hands on in the supermarket because you have had a hard day at work, the children are irritable, or you are feeling unwell. When you get home, you discover you have bought the one brand of baked beans that nobody likes, or that the 'quick casserole' actually requires three ingredients you've never even heard of, never mind got in the cupboard!

Emotional exhaustion can have a very numbing effect, causing you to feel unable to think about alternatives. In any changing situation, give yourself time to talk together about what is happening. It can be helpful to write down all the ways you might deal with the coming change, discussing those you could easily accept, and those you definitely couldn't. This will not necessarily wipe out disagreements, but you will be able to see a broader range of ideas than you might have done at first.

For you to try – what responses do you use most often?

This exercise is to help you decide which responses you usually favour when facing change. Think back to the last time you had to face change. It could be something you faced together as a couple, or perhaps a change you encountered as an individual. Using the 'helpful and unhelpful responses' we looked at just now, think back to the way you handled the change:

- At the beginning, when the need for change began to be apparent, did you try to push the thoughts under the carpet, or did you attempt to make sense of them somehow? What was the result of your approach?
- As you took decisions about the issue you were dealing with, did you blame your partner (or others) for the decisions you made? Did you blame yourself if things went wrong?
- After the change had been worked through, did you feel content with the outcome? Do you still feel you could have done more, or that your partner did not fully understand?
- What action resulted from the responses and decisions you made? Did this action reflect the true needs of the situation? Did the result only go part way towards your expectations?

Once you have thought through this exercise, you may be able to see a pattern emerge that demonstrates how you usually deal with change. For instance, are there particular stress points at certain stages of the 'change circle'? Do you handle action better than preparation? Are you more at ease when turning things over in your mind, but fear to take positive steps forward? If there is a pattern, think about harnessing your insight to consider whether there might be more ways to use 'helpful' responses, instead of 'unhelpful' responses, in the future.

The value of change

Change can be confusing and tiring, but can also be exhilarating and enlivening. Imagine filling a pond with clear, sparkling water and stocking it with goldfish. At first, you sit beside it and enjoy the cool water. Over time, though, the pool begins to stagnate and the fish die. So you avoid visiting it, and eventually dig it up altogether. Relationships that have no change are like this – they don't bubble, and have no excitement. Couples caught in these relationships find it harder and harder to give time and attention to their partnership because it can seem dispiriting to think about doing anything. Eventually they may 'cut and run', because the prospect of starting from scratch again is so daunting.

Change can be a catalyst to an improved relationship.

Case history
Brendan and Janet discovered this for themselves when Janet broke her leg. Unfortunately, the break was a bad one, and Janet spent several months in treatment. She was unable to go to work, or do the jobs around the home that she normally did. At first, Janet felt upset that she could not do things as usual. She especially enjoyed cooking, and had always done the cooking for the family, so it was a real blow to her to give up preparing meals. She also privately felt that Brendan and their two daughters would not be up to cooking to her standard. To her surprise, the family rallied round, and as time went on she began to look forward to the unusual meals that Brendan and the girls served up. She gradually saw that in taking full responsibility for the cooking, she had denied them the creative fun of making a meal. Once her leg was better, she explained how much she enjoyed sharing the cooking. They then went on to explore different types of food, and had a lot of fun cooking together.

For Brendan and Janet, what could have been a potentially difficult situation served to enrich their family life. It takes courage to embrace change, but it can have many rewards if handled effectively. In the following chapters we will be looking at handling change at specific points in a relationship, and the special needs the couple may have at these times.

2
The Growing Relationship

The precise ways in which couples handle change is an individual matter. However, the rolling cycle of change has definite stages, and you may be able to identify these in your own relationships. The different stages can occur at any point in a relationship – regardless of whether you have known each other just a few weeks or been married for 50 years.

When I first meet couples whom I am to counsel, I often begin by asking them about the early days of the relationship. I do this because it can help me to start to understand what the 'basics' might be for this particular couple. It can also offer the couple some time to reflect on what *first* brought them together – which in some cases may have been many years before. Many couples are amazed to rediscover what first drew them together, and often comment on the remembered closeness of this time. Watching them, I can often see a vivid reflection of their early days. Their faces change! Often they smile, or exchange warm glances with each other, even before they begin to reply to my question. They may be in the middle of an unhappy time, but somehow this memory of their first meeting recalls great pleasure. It is only later that couples begin to describe difficulties creeping into their relationship. It is not uncommon for couples who are still at the early stage of their relationship to cope easily with problems that seem insurmountable later.

Case history
Jill and Mike were like this. When they first met they were on holiday in Devon, camping with friends. During the two weeks they spent together, they felt very close. Both had a strong sense that the relationship was destined to be special. Although they lived a long way apart, they spent the following months travelling to visit one another. They also wrote long letters, and phoned frequently. The distance between them seemed to increase their longing to be together, and made every meeting very exciting. Mike was finally able to transfer his job to be nearer to Jill, and they married 18 months after first meeting. All went well, until Jill was asked to work away from home for long periods. She was able to come home at weekends, but their relationship began to suffer. Neither felt close to the other, and all the excitement they had enjoyed at meeting after

a time apart seemed to have melted away. They were both aware of a change in the way they related, but were unable to say exactly what had changed for them.

Jill and Mike reflect what is true for most relationships. As they grow, both in actual time and emotional maturity, they pass through specific stages, each carrying their special pleasures and problems. This process begins when a couple meet, and can continue until a relationship moves on to greater commitment, or parting. As you read the following stages, see if your own experiences fit the pattern of new relationships.

Stage 1   Meeting someone new

Meeting a new partner can appear to be a simple act, and perhaps irrelevant to your surroundings or background. In reality, where and how you meet your new partner can provide both of you with many hidden messages about the nature of the relationship to come. For instance, where you meet may accurately reflect your interests, or be a coincidence that tells your prospective partner very little about the real you. You might go to the same night club every Saturday evening because the club is the centre of your social life, and you know lots of people there, or you may be at the club because your friends persuaded you to come along, and you really want to go home. It is easy to make assumptions at this stage, which you will need to check out later. First impressions can often give a clue to the nature of the person you meet, but can sometimes be inaccurate. Couples often tell me they met under very unfavourable circumstances, but managed to overcome these to discover more about each other.

Useful skills at stage 1
When you first make contact with someone you may want to get to know better, think about what is attracting you:

Is it looks, or personality? Is it a mixture of both, or weighted in one direction? Have you been influenced by where you met, or even the opinion of a friend? Try to draw out the person to whom you are attracted, and listen to what they talk about. Do they seem to hide thoughts and feelings behind a need to impress, or can they discuss a variety of subjects with reasonable ease? If someone shows a powerful interest in you, it can knock out your normal defences and cause you to enter into a friendship more deeply and more quickly than is normal for you. Of course, feeling attractive to your partner is important, but, if you feel flattered by another's approaches, try to decide whether you really like them, or are responding to a deeper need within you to be thought likeable.

Stage 2   Getting to know your partner

This stage in a relationship can be the most exciting, but also the most nerve-racking! As you build up a picture of the person you are going out with, you may become acutely aware that they are also building a picture of you. You are probably keen to present your best 'face', and might even choose to hide parts of you that seem less attractive, both physically and emotionally. It can be tempting to keep parts of your life private, and in some circumstances this is wise.

For instance, if you are divorced or separated, introducing your children to every new friendship runs the risk of confusing and hurting them. Even when you are uncertain about the future of a particular relationship, your children may become attached to your new partner. They may then have to cope with losing another adult they care about, especially if you have not been separated from their mother or father for long. It may simply be enough to say to your prospective boy- or girlfriend that you are separated, with children, until you feel more certain of this new relationship.

How your prospective partner sees you depends on how much of your inner self you choose to share. You may find it easy to talk, and tell your partner everything, or be naturally more reserved. Judging the timing of discussing personal issues can be a fine art. It can feel overwhelming to hear another's life story during the first date. However, you do need to begin to discover how compatible the two of you are likely to be by sharing at least some of the 'real' you. This can feel a little risky, but if you mask the deeper side of you too effectively, the relationship may never feel comfortable. You may end up feeling afraid that if your partner finds the 'real' you, they will leave.

Useful skills at stage 2

Studies show that people who share similar values and beliefs are likely to form lasting relationships. They are also likely to share the same interests and hobbies – an interest in similar types of music, for instance. (The old adage about opposites attracting can be true, but a relationship made entirely of opposite opinions will also be fiery, and can crumble easily if a crisis hits.) Talk to your new partner about anything that is important to you. It might be something as potentially contentious as politics, or as simple as your favourite foods. This helps you to construct a rounded view of your new friend, and offers them a chance to learn about you, before you move on to the next stage. You should watch for warning signs of impending problems. Any signs of aggression, jealousy or harassment should be treated seriously. Do not imagine you will be *the* one to save this person – they need to deal with their own insecurities before they are ready to commit themselves in a relationship.

Stage 3   Getting deeper

By this stage, you are likely to have gained a real sense of your partner as a whole person. By now, you will have formed an opinion about their looks and personality. If you have decided that the relationship is right to invest in, you may be entering the phase that many people feel is the best of times. You will feel intensely attracted to your new partner, and spend all your time apart looking forward to meeting up again. Your partner may appear to have all the attributes you have ever wanted in a man or woman. Some people even experience a sense of euphoria and well-being that can have an almost addictive quality.

At around this time, you are likely to consider the sexual side of your relationship. Although this may seem a natural progression, it is worth thinking about whether you are ready for a sexual relationship, and what you in fact mean by 'a sexual relationship'. What it means to you may not be what your partner means. A useful analogy for sex in relationships can be to think about sex as being like a swimming pool. If you charge into the pool, and immediately dive off the diving board into the deep end, you only have two options – you can sink or swim. You might splutter to the side, feeling frightened, vowing never to be so foolish again. Or you could relish the experience, and rush quickly back up the stairs, perhaps missing the pleasures of swimming more slowly. Whichever option, you will have had little time to reflect on your feelings, and will probably be forced into this very polarized view of diving. However, if you paddle gently up from the shallow end, you can acclimatize to the depth and temperature of the water. You can decide if you want to risk going a little deeper, or move back to the shallow end. You may eventually decide to dive in, but you will have had time to get ready for this decision. Many people imagine that beginning a sexual relationship is a sink or swim situation, when actually you can give yourself time to decide what you really want. Like the swimming pool, you can enjoy a sexual relationship just as much by reflecting on how intimate a relationship you want, and then testing out your feelings.

Useful skills at stage 3

You may feel swept along by the excitement of your new relationship, but try to use this stage to look at what you are enjoying together. Are you going along to his stock-car racing every Saturday, or her favourite folk music club, because you genuinely enjoy these activities and want to share them, or because you like the *idea* of liking them? Falling for somebody can often blind you to your own true preferences. It can even cause you to defend behaviour in your partner that you would condemn in someone else. You may also find yourself more deeply committed than you expected if your partnership is opposed by others. This may sound contradictory, but opposition from parents, relatives or friends can cause a couple to cling tightly together – rather like gripping on to your partner as you battle through a howling gale. In this situation, you are less likely to make an objective assessment of your partner than if your choice is generally approved.

Sexually speaking, it may seem calculating to dissect your feelings, but it can save you much heartache in the future. Try to decide if the relationship should be sexual at all and, if it is, what boundaries are right for you. It might help to write down your thoughts before facing a situation where you have to make a decision. You should take some questions very seriously indeed. The use of 'safe sex' practices, and contraceptives, should be at the top of your list. No matter how passionate your relationship, you cannot afford the risk of an unwanted pregnancy or a sexually transmitted disease. You should also consider whether you really want the sexual relationship at all, or are being persuaded in some way. If there is any suggestion of aggression or force, the relationship could be heading for serious difficulties, and you could be badly hurt. Emotional blackmail can be equally dangerous. If you are asked to have sex because 'it proves you love me', or 'I'll leave you if you don't', you should consider if the relationship is worth having on these grounds.

Stage 4   Into reality

As you move through the intense romantic stage I have described in stage 3, you will notice changes beginning to occur in the way you see your partner. How long you stay at stage 3 is variable, and can last some months in one relationship, but only a few weeks in another. Eventually, you will move on. For many couples, this can be 'make your mind up time'! From the 'high' of feeling that your partner is perfect in every way, you may begin to notice certain things that annoy or irritate you.

Case history
Avril and Connor felt this way. They had met at a friend's house, and gradually got to know each other over a period of several months. Although their relationship had been slow to start, they became inseparable. Connor belonged to the local Amateur Dramatic Society, so Avril too joined the group. Avril was less outgoing than Connor, but she admired his confidence with others, and his ability to talk to anybody about his acting. Connor found Avril's shyness attractive, and liked the way that she listened to people without always blowing her own trumpet.

After a while, though, Connor noticed he sometimes felt frustrated with Avril. He wanted her to talk to his friends, and felt that she came over as 'standoffish' by saying so little. Avril had also begun to wonder if Connor was genuinely sharing his enjoyment of acting, or 'just being bigheaded' when he held forth on the society's latest play.

Avril and Connor had met the 'reality crunch'. Because the romantic phase can feel so exciting, the less acceptable side of your partner can be masked. As the heady first feelings fade, so other aspects show through. It is rather as if seeing someone through a veil (either of their making, or one you wanted them to wear), and then having this veil torn away. There may be nothing sinister about what you suddenly notice; comparatively mild things can seem important – like your partner's choice of hairstyle, or the way they eat. As with Avril and Connor, what initially attracted you may suddenly take on a less attractive side. Being with someone who seems the life and soul of the party can turn to embarrassment when they do not seem to understand that their jokes might upset others. Quietness may seem flattering when it suggests your partner is listening attentively, but is less acceptable if you feel they are not able to hold a conversation with you.

It is important to remember that these feelings are natural, and do not necessarily mean you should end the relationship. Most relationships are unable to sustain the peaks of stage 3 for ever. Eventually, they need to descend to the foothills of normal life to see if the relationship can cope with the knocks of reality. Seeing your partner in a more realistic light can help to strengthen your partnership, and prove vital to the building of the all-important 'basics' we discussed in Chapter 1.

Useful skills at stage 4

You may feel that if you can see faults in your partner, then you are not really in love. This is far from the truth; it is simply that the way in which you love your partner is changing. If you can both survive this stage, then your relationship will be the stronger for it.

However, this 'reality crunch' can tell you some important things about your relationship. Try to assess what it is you have begun to feel is less than perfect about your partner:

- Are your doubts connected to their looks or dress sense? Or perhaps whether they have an expensive car, or great taste in restaurants? If you feel concerned about this, the relationship may be based on what others think, rather than your own values and concerns. If these things are important to you, then your relationships may struggle to make a greater commitment, as you may both be afraid of exposing your inner self.
- Perhaps your partner's behaviour bothers you? It might be that the nights you used to enjoy at the local pub now seem boring, especially if your partner ends up getting drunk every time. Perhaps the way your partner's friends exclude you is difficult to take, when previously you have tolerated this. Ask yourself if you could live with this behaviour over a long period. Don't tell yourself this behaviour will change if you love your partner enough. It may, but it would be dangerous to build a relationship on this possibility.
- Are you more concerned about your partner's relatives, children or ex-partners than the relationship itself? How others respond to you can have an enormous influence on a relationship. What previously pushed you together may also have the potential to pull you apart. If her sister won't speak to you, it may initially feel like a mild annoyance. It could be a big headache in the future, though, if you can't change her opinion of you.
- Are there cultural and ethnic differences that should be considered? Cross-cultural relationships can often be rich in understanding and tolerance; and many couples who get together across religious and colour boundaries develop relationships that are strong. However, they may have had to work extra hard at overcoming prejudice, and there is no doubt that such relationships have to have a 100 per cent commitment to make these differences work *for* the partnership rather than *against* it. Before reaching stage 4, these differences may

seem conquerable by love alone. However, the 'reality crunch' will often highlight these problems in a dramatic way, and can be characterized by rows over religion or the traditional ways that men or women are treated in relationships.

In all of these areas, talking honestly about potential areas of conflict will help a great deal in pre-empting the sudden blow of recognizing just how different your expectations are. It can help to ask yourself, 'What is the worst that could happen?' If you can face the most difficult scenario together, then you can feel prepared for less unhappy situations.

Stage 5   Coming back up

Once you have reached stage 4, you may wonder if your relationship can survive at all! Sometimes couples marry, or move in together, at stage 3, and then break up because stage 4 feels so different to the romance of earlier times. They will have fallen prey to the idea that acknowledging the less attractive side of the relationship means it must be over. A relationship that never passes through times of self-questioning can never grow, and often cannot withstand the challenge of change.

Gradually you will begin to notice that the strong feelings of irritation about your partner's habits or behaviour start to fade. It is likely that during stage 4 you will both have talked about the issues you have found tricky. You have probably argued, or even had trial separations. You might feel that these experiences have eventually brought you closer to one another, and enabled you to know each other better. Alternatively, you may feel the relationship cannot be sustained – that the differences between you are just too great.

If you stay together

If you have been able to weather the storms of stage 4, you have probably begun to rediscover the good things about each other you knew at the beginning of your relationship. You could even find yourselves making a special effort to visit places you first went to when you got together, or weaving in new experiences. This can seem like a relief, and a time of consolidation, after the highs and lows of earlier times. One of the great pleasures of this can be the real sense of depth that your relationship may now have. You have seen the worst sides of each other, but you also know how you both cope with problems, and this can be extremely reassuring. Another bonus is the sense of humour that can emerge at this point. Your partner's disastrous haircut, or the row with his mother, can now develop a sense of perspective, and may even seem funny in retrospect. Many family stories develop from this – and can make you both laugh long after the event.

In other words, instead of the false picture of the perfect partner, or the worst partner, you will have a picture of you partner that is a mixture of these – that is, a *whole* person. Your partner will also have gone through the same process with you, so that the relationship can be integrated – that is, neither weighted to one side nor the other. If you can see your partner as having strengths and vulnerabilities in different areas, you can forgive and support them more easily. You can also ask your partner to use their strengths to help you with things you find more difficult than they do, and you can do the same for them.

Case history

Wesley and Sammie felt this way about their relationship. They had been together for about ten months, and each had gradually learnt more about the other. They had been attracted to each other by a mutual interest in helping at the local community centre. Wesley led a youth group there, while Sammie helped out at an aerobics class. At first, Sammie saw Wesley's youth group help as an illustration of his community spirit. They met with a 'reality crunch', though, when Sammie began to feel that Wesley paid more attention to his group than her, especially on Friday nights when she wanted to go out. Wesley began to wonder if Sammie was right for him, if she couldn't accept his involvement at the community centre.

At first they argued, but then Wesley explained to Sammie that he had become involved with the group after his cousin died from a drug overdose. He had felt helpless, and decided that helping young people to stay off the streets, and encouraging them to feel more positive about their lives, might be a way of coping with his cousin's death. Sammie was then better able to appreciate Wesley's involvement, and understood his need to help at the club. She saw the vulnerable side of Wesley – the part that had been hurt by his cousin's death. Although he was no longer on the pedestal she had created for him as a 'selfless pillar of the community', she felt more able to support him in his work.

Eventually, they were able to create a compromise so that they went out together some Fridays, and Wesley went to the club on another day. Their relationship was different because of the change in the way they saw each other. They found themselves more prepared to cope with difficult circumstances because they could be honest with each other, without the strain of trying to maintain an image of the other that was false. Wesley could be free to make mistakes, because Sammie no longer saw him as perfect, while Sammie felt Wesley would be willing to support her when she needed his help.

If you decide to part

Sometimes the crunch of stage 4 can cause a couple to feel they cannot go on together. This is often because learning about their partner causes them to see aspects they know they can never come to terms with, even if they work really hard at the relationship. Usually these problems are connected to deeper issues than the way a partner looks, or irritating habits. Usually, fundamental difficulties will come to the surface, perhaps to do with personal beliefs, or different approaches to sex or money. Any arguments are likely to result in a kind of 'stonewalling' from either partner (that is, a refusal to discuss the problem in any depth, and a denial of personal responsibility). The realization that the relationship is not going to last may be sudden, or there may be a gradual understanding that nothing can be done to make the partnership last.

Useful skills at stage 5

Reflecting on your partnership is helpful at this point. Do you feel able to build on the relationship so far, or does it feel as if you keep having to start from scratch each time you meet? Your relationship 'foundations' will begin to settle at this time. A feeling that you have to keep going over the same ground may mean you have little to draw on as the relationship progresses.

Think about how you argue. Arguments that may feel fierce can be useful if some positive action comes at the end of them. If your disagreements seem to bring up the same topics repeatedly, or end with nothing being done to solve the problem, then you need to discuss what is blocking you from both reaching a decision. (Of course, rows that involve aggression and violence do not solve problems, and usually make any existing problem worse.) The block might be something you can work on yourself, such as a fear of being seen in the wrong, but it could be deeper. You might feel you will never agree, because you come from totally different positions. These 'poles apart' disagreements are commonly linked to differences in the way you handle certain situations. As Chapter 1 showed, the way in which your family dealt with emotions can influence your own approach. If you and your partner come from families who have completely opposing attitudes, then you will struggle to find neutral ground. In a sense, you have to use your own pair of emotional scales, and weigh up whether the effort of building effective communication in the relationship outweighs the problems you have met.

In general, though, you can use stage 5 to enjoy each other's company, and relax in the knowledge that you can trust your partner. This is perhaps the goal of most relationships – the desire to trust another, and to feel trusted in return. The sense of security that this kind of relationship offers can be a base for discovering new things about yourself and others. Some people may suggest that this type of relationship is boring and too 'safe', but relationships that offer security can be innovative, and stand much risk-taking that other relationships cannot bear. You can be free to disagree, share your deepest thoughts, expose the side of you that no one else knows about, and work through the cycles of change that may lie ahead.

How the different stages may affect your sexual relationship

As your general relationship grows and changes, so your sexual relationship will alter. At first, the sex is likely to be passionate and all-consuming. You may pay little attention to technique, and feel carried away by the pleasure. This is likely to cause you to feel that not only is your partner the most wonderful person, but also the best lover in the world! Even if there are problems with sex – perhaps lack of orgasm, or erectile difficulties – your desire to see only the best in your partner may cause you to blank out the difficulty.

As the relationship progresses, you may become more critical of the type of sex you are sharing. You may decide your partner wants too much sex, or too little. You may begin to feel that your needs are not being considered, or that your partner demands too much of you. It is also possible to believe that because the exciting, effortless sex of the earlier stage has changed to sex that requires more attention and understanding, this means that the relationship is doomed. (There are some people who move from relationship to relationship as soon as the sex changes, rather as a butterfly flits from flower to flower. Essentially, they never allow themselves to discover the way in which a relationship can change and grow over time.)

Negotiating and talking about sex together can lead on to greater pleasure and enjoyment because you can both ask for what pleases you, and develop a willingness to experiment together. This sharing has a double-sided effect. It can improve your love life, but also help you both to feel closer and more sensitive to each other. Once your relationship has gone through the earlier stages, and come through successfully, you may notice a deepening in your sexual fulfilment. The developing trust can give sex a profound sense of satisfaction. This satisfaction will be quite different to the transitory passion of early on in the relationship, but helps to create a bond that many couples find enriching.

All relationships pass through these phases, although you may not always notice this. Sometimes the phases blur into each other, or one stage may seem less important than another. It is also true to say that these stages are often repeated throughout the life of a relationship. Difficult situations, or even simply growing older together, can reactivate feelings of disillusionment, or renewed closeness. Understanding that this is part of the way in which relationships change and mature can be helpful. You are less likely to experience feelings of anxiety or insecurity if you can see the pattern of the five stages outlined in this chapter. You may also be more willing to work on the relationship if you have understood the way in which one stage leads to another.

To describe a relationship as 'growing' is very apt in making sense of the ups and downs of the life of a relationship. In the same way that trees spurt ahead during the growing season, slow down in periods of drought or cold, or break into life after seeming to be dead, relationships pass through seasons of change. The patterns of new relationships described in this chapter are part of the growth necessary to all relationships.

3

Children, and Their Impact on Your Relationship

For many couples, the change associated with parenthood is probably the greatest, and most difficult, they have to undertake. Sometimes the impact of change ahead can be sensed long before children actually arrive on the scene – or a choice is made to become parents at all. Many couples making a commitment to a long-term relationship still assume parenthood to be part of their plans for the future, although an increasing number of people are questioning this automatic assumption and see the possibility of parenthood as just one of a range of options. There are others who hope and expect to have a family, only to find their plans dashed as they discover they are suffering from fertility problems. The potential for change in all these situations is clear, but handling the changes of deciding to have children, and coping with them as part of your relationship, can seem confusing and complex. This chapter aims to look at some of the most common problems encountered concerning parenthood, and how to approach these in order to make decisions that build up your relationship rather than undermine it.

Planning for parenthood

Deciding to have a child can be a rich mixture of emotion, practical considerations and pressure from outside your partnership. As with other types of change, there are helpful and unhelpful ways of thinking about making this decision. You can use the 'helpful' and 'unhelpful' responses from Chapter 1 to see how choosing parenthood can be helped or hindered.

Unhelpful responses

1 It can be tempting to deny the need to think and talk about parenthood at all. I see many couples who tell me that one or all of their children are 'mistakes' – that is, not previously discussed or planned. While some couples cope well with unplanned pregnancy and childbirth, many find themselves set up for arguments later about feeling manipulated, or overstretched financially, by this approach. Many teenage pregnancies occur because of this. It is as if

one partner, or both, tell themselves that if they don't think about pregnancy, the responsibility will go away. Denial is dangerous because it prevents any possibility of choice, which is vital to you, your partner and, ultimately, your child.

2 You may notice that you find it difficult to discuss having children. There may be a part of you that avoids the subject because it feels unromantic to talk so cold-bloodedly about having, or not having, a child. Or you may sense that the subject has the potential to develop into a row – perhaps because one of you is for the idea of having a baby, and the other is against. If you avoid discussing the issue in this way, it may simmer beneath the surface of a relationship, boiling up into arguments that never seem to reach resolution.

3 You may find you end up shifting the responsibility for the decision on to each other, or someone else completely. Some men may say that any decision to have a child has to be the woman's alone, because she has to carry the baby during pregnancy and give birth. A couple may decide to have a child because one of their parents 'wants a grandchild', or because they have friends of a similar age who have started a family. While all of these have relevance in the decision-making process, they may cause a couple to resent each other, or the child, if they are the sole reason for having a baby.

Helpful responses

1 Acknowledgement and acceptance are important elements in making this key decision about your lives together. Admitting you need to talk, and sharing your own sense of responsibility in the decision, opens the way for you to explore a range of options. Even if the pregnancy comes about as an accident, you can still utilize these skills to help you decide about your needs in the future.

2 If you can remain flexible as you talk through the possibility of parenthood, you will both be able to accommodate each other's anxieties and expectations. If one of you comes to the discussion with solidly fixed ideas – that you should try for a baby in two months' time, for example – you may find that neither of you can express the deeper concerns you need to share. You may be so busy discussing whether it should be two months or six, that you do not tackle the all-important decision about whether to be parents at all!

3 No decision is set in concrete. Yet it is not unusual for people to believe that changing your mind is somehow a sign of weakness, or an indecisive personality. Actually, the ability to reassess any situation, and adapt to changing need, can be a source of strength to a partnership. This skill is very important for planned parenthood

because of the obvious difficulty about stopping a pregnancy once started. If you have changing circumstances, then you need to be able to reassess your decision to have, or not have, a child before a pregnancy occurs.

For you to try – Decision aids

1 Find time to talk when you know you can be alone together. Don't try to make this kind of decision in a group of friends at the local pub, or when you are both concentrating on something else, like a video, or late at night when you have both had a hard day at work. These may sound unlikely times to talk, but I see many couples who attempt to make serious decisions in just these circumstances.

2 Spend some time drawing up a 'for' and 'against' list. Note everything you can think of, from 'I don't like smelly nappies' to 'My childhood wasn't great – how will I be able to give my child a better one?' Some important ideas to consider might be your financial situation, accommodation, future plans, 'gut feelings' (like worries about knowing how to deal with a baby), and your general health. Compare your lists (or do one together), and talk through each issue. Some may balance each other out, or seem unimportant once you've discussed them. Others you will need to take action on – like stopping smoking or drinking. Whatever happens, you will both be coming to your decision understanding your partner more, and with greater consensus.

3 Remember, or write down, the issues that need working on. Don't put them aside and forget about them. Create time when you can discuss these regularly, but don't nag your partner for a decision when they cannot give one immediately. You will both need personal space to think about your feelings and thoughts without feeling pressurized.

The pressures on your relationship

1 Pregnancy

The discovery of pregnancy can create subtle changes in a relationship, some of which can be an apt preparation for becoming parents, while others create stress in a partnership. It is likely that the woman will need more support and concern than ever before, and although her partner may be very willing to give this, he may feel under pressure to live up to her changing expectations. Because pregnancy itself is a state of constant change, both partners may find it hard to explain what their needs are at any one time. The woman may be well aware of her physical and emotional changes, but uncertain how to share these with her partner, especially if her partner seems preoccupied by other concerns. There may also be a growing awareness that 'this is for real' – sometimes linked to the change in size of the woman as her pregnancy progresses. This can help a couple come to terms in a gradual way with the changes that a baby will bring. However, if a couple have doubts about their partnership, this growing realization of parenthood can be extremely challenging, and may result in feelings of entrapment or confusion about the basis for the relationship. Some couples have a 'romantic' view of pregnancy and babies, which can be severely knocked by the woman's morning sickness and midnight trips to the loo! This can be helpful in that the couple have a chance to practise their response to some of the realities of parenthood, but also difficult as their personal ideals are challenged. Of course, concerns about not becoming pregnant when you both hoped you would conceive easily can also be problematic. Some of these issues are discussed later in this chapter under 'Deciding not to have children, or when you find you can't'.

Case history
Patrick and Mary had been married for three years when they discovered that Mary was pregnant. They had hoped to start a family one day, but had not planned to have a child quite so soon in their marriage. They were both worried about how they would manage financially, as they were already on a tight budget. Neither of them wanted to raise these uncertain feelings. Patrick avoided discussing his concerns with Mary because he did not want to hurt her when he knew she would be feeling especially vulnerable. Mary avoided telling Patrick how worried *she* was because she thought Patrick would be unhappy if she admitted her worries.

Several weeks passed, and Mary and Patrick found themselves hardly discussing the pregnancy at all. Then Mary began to bleed, and was taken into hospital for observation. The crisis seemed to break their communication deadlock, and they blurted out all their mixed emotions to each other as Mary lay in the hospital bed. The anxiety about having the baby was now heightened by anxiety about losing it, and this released the dam of blocked feelings they were both holding back. Neither of them fully realized how their lack of communication had prevented them from giving and receiving support from each other at such a difficult point in their lives. Fortunately, Mary did not lose the baby, and although Patrick and

Mary still faced some problems about becoming a family, they were far more able to face these together once they aired their mutual feelings.

Useful skills at this stage

- Try keeping a journal of your feelings and thoughts throughout the pregnancy. I am not suggesting that either of you write a novel, but you could use a few words to describe how you are feeling at any given time. Something like 'tired today', 'felt elated when the baby first moved', or 'feel worried we won't cope with night feeds', could be sufficient.

- Use your journals to discuss the week, or as pointers to your own feelings, and then share your thoughts. A useful aid to dealing with problems at this point might be 'reframing' (see Chapter 1). For instance, sex can seem increasingly problematic as the woman's shape changes. Instead of seeing this as negative, you could use this as a chance to explore other ways of enjoying sexual contact that you may have forgotten, or never tried. You could also boost your affection level with cuddles and hugs, which will increase a sense of closeness for both of you.

- Inform yourself about the process of pregnancy and childbirth. Although you may feel nervous about these things, knowledge can help dispel such feelings. *Ask questions!* Doctors, midwives and hospital staff should be able to help you make sense of all you have to deal with. This can help you feel like a 'team' rather than just two individuals, which is an important skill to learn as you become parents. If you feel you don't understand, or have been sidelined in a medical decision, keep asking until you feel satisfied.

2   Babies and toddlers

The arrival of a baby in a couple's relationship can be the equivalent of a friendly explosion! On the one hand, there is the delight and pleasure that babies usually bring with them: on the other, there is often a sense that nothing will be the same again – from the endless piles of washing to the doubts about ever being a 'good enough' parent.

Perhaps if a couple have tried for a baby for a long time, their joyful feelings will be uppermost. However, if the baby was unplanned, and money is already tight, the couple may feel extremely ambivalent about the new arrival. Even in families where the baby is welcomed, and the relationship is steady, the inevitability of change can feel hard to handle. It is sometimes easier to appreciate and understand the need for change in unhappy circumstances (such as divorce or bereavement) than it is to see the need in something that most people tend to see as a happy event, such as having a baby. But babies can bring new kinds of stress in a relationship; and it is because this pressure is new and different from other kinds of stressful situations that the couple have learnt to handle in the past, that they need to be especially aware of their own needs as partners, as well as new parents.

Useful skills at this stage

- A new baby can seem all-consuming, but you need to give time and attention to each other as well. If your couple relationship is put aside for your new baby, you may drift into being emotionally distant from each other. Children need parents who give them consistent care, but who are also fulfilled themselves – and this is also true for single parents. It is easy to become resentful if a child seems to take over your whole life and prevents you from enjoying your own interests, or simply denies you a life of your own. Once the early, most demanding months are over, and you settle into more of a routine, make time just for you. At first, it might just be ten minutes of peace with a cup of tea, or a shared favourite television programme. At first, don't be too ambitious by booking whole evenings out unless you are really confident, as you may find you need to build up to this amount of time together.

- Use the time available to you productively, rather than sticking to old patterns of shared time. For instance, you may have always spent time together in the evenings after a meal, but now find this is just the moment that your baby chooses to wake up and cry! If you cannot be together during the day, then think how you might use shared time more effectively. Perhaps you could avoid cooking big meals, and instead choose something simpler that does not keep you in the kitchen for hours on end.

- Utilize the support networks available to you. Some new parents feel they must take full responsibility for everything, and feel guilty if they need to ask for help. This approach compares with being asked to do a completely new job, with little training, and feeling embarrassed to ask someone how to work the machinery! You can seek support from various sources. You can get formal support from professionals such as your local midwife or antenatal clinic, doctors and social services. There are also many voluntary agencies who can help with parenting, so investigate your local centres for these (see Helping Agencies list at back of book). You can also use your informal support network. Your family and friends may be rich sources of help – from baby-sitting, to somewhere to let off steam!

- Don't forget to boost each other's self-esteem. You may both feel as if you are locked into automatic pilot, doing daily tasks just to get through another day. A hug, a kind remark, or a small token of care from and to your partner, can help you both feel cared for at a time when you are having to give out a lot of emotional energy to a small baby. Affection can be the oil that keeps the wheels turning in a relationship, and can help as a gentle reintroduction to a sexual relationship.

3   School-age children

The point at which children go to school can be a time of change for most parents. After the intense work of bringing up a baby, where you make all the decisions about upbringing, some parents find it very hard to give their child into the responsibility of someone else. It can also alter the way in which you see yourself as a mother or father. It may be that being with your child has given you a sense of self-esteem or routine, so that when a child attends school (or sometimes playschool) for the first time, you feel uncertain about your role. If you have other children at home, this feeling may not be so great, but can seem worse when your last child starts school. Increasing numbers of parents face this feeling much earlier than schooldays if they use a childminder or nursery school.

Case history
Sally and Matthew had enjoyed looking after their son, Luke, as he grew from a baby to a lively 3-year-old. As Sally had the better-paid job, they had decided that Matthew would stay at home with their son. Matthew gave up his job, and soon relished the role of main carer for his young son. Sally and Matthew had decided during Sally's pregnancy that they would like Luke to go to nursery school when he was 3; and when Luke was a year old they put his name down on the waiting list of the local nursery school. At first Matthew enjoyed taking Luke to the school. He appeared to settle down well, but then Luke began to cry for his father, and on one occasion the school called Matthew to collect his son, who was very upset.

Matthew tried to talk to Sally about his sadness at leaving Luke at the nursery when he seemed so miserable, but Sally did not appear to take much notice of Matthew's remarks, often brushing him off by saying that Luke was 'just going through a bad phase'. Eventually Matthew accused Sally of not caring about him and Luke, and they had a big row. For a few days, communication was very strained between them. But then Sally apologized, saying that she now realized she hadn't really understood the importance of Matthew's worries about Luke. Together they began to talk about the issue, and decided to go together to discuss the problem with Luke's nursery teacher. This was very successful, as they were able to plan strategies jointly to help Luke feel more settled at school.

When your child is cared for by others

- Prepare for your child moving out of your full-time care by reassuring yourself about where they are going, and what the 'basics' are that must be met for both you and your partner to feel confident about your child's safety and growth. Visit schools and nurseries more than once, and get a feel for the atmosphere. Talk to other parents and staff, asking questions that are important to you. It is helpful to talk over with your partner those things that you both regard as vital, and those matters that might be compromised on. If you are choosing a childminder, use a registered one, and visit the location where your child will be cared for.
- You may feel a loss of control over a child, but this is natural, and will happen anyway as a child matures. Sometimes, uncomfortable emotions connected to a child leaving the home base may be because the balance of the couple relationship has shifted. Having the child around may have deflected you from appreciating the changes in your relationship, but once the child starts to move out into the world, you may begin to realize all too clearly the work needing to be done on the relationship. You can avoid this by giving your partnership time, as well as caring for your child.
- When children meet and socialize with others of their own age, you may also find that you and your partner argue over matters of discipline. Your child will be learning other ways of seeing the world, and testing these new discoveries on both of you. You may also notice that your child tries to play you off against one another, or comes to you both for different matters. You may wonder why it is always you that has to get up in the middle of the night, and not your partner, or why you child only wants your partner to play certain games or read a goodnight story. It may be easier to accept some of these changes than others, but, as with all change, you may feel your relationship strained in certain areas. It is common for partners to feel unsupported in dealing with children of this age, and arguments can develop as you both face differences in your expectations over your child's behaviour. Some of these differences may be linked to your own upbringing, and a desire to give your

child the same sort of background that you had – or perhaps even a feeling that you want to do things completely differently.

Agreeing on upbringing

- Discuss your personal views before you reach a crisis. Make a list of the scenarios you might face, and discuss how you would both handle them. For instance, your child asks to stay the night at a friend's house, someone you do not know personally. What would you both need to know in order to make a decision? Would your child need to be a certain age in order to do this? Do you feel strongly enough to say 'my child would never be allowed to do this', or 'maybe, in certain circumstances'?

- If your child does something you feel is completely against your code, agree with your partner a course of action. If you take action alone, you run the risk of your partner disagreeing, and refusing to back your decision. You may then end up fighting each other, rather than dealing with the problem. Of course, some things will need dealing with immediately, and when you are by yourself, so talk over how you might handle minor difficulties ahead of time.

  For instance, your child leaves their toys all over the room after playing with them. Do you think they should clear them up? Or do you think *you* should, because he or she is not old enough to tidy them up properly? Or should you and the child do it together?

- As your children grow older, ask them what they think is appropriate behaviour in certain situations. This sounds risky, and to some extent it is, but listening to your child can help you both make decisions that are workable, rather than ones imposed from above.

4 Teenagers

Teenagers can have a devastating effect on family life, and on the most stable of couples. This is mainly because they tend to remind the adult 'you' of your own teens, and the confusion of physical and emotional changes you probably went through at the time. The teens are also a time of testing what has previously been acceptable, and this can be very frustrating for parents who thought they had just learnt how to handle tricky situations. Many couples find themselves polarized by a teenager in a way they could not have predicted.

Teenagers can also upset the sexual equilibrium between partners, simply because of their powerful emerging sexuality. Couples who see me for psychosexual therapy tell me that their teenagers have often made them feel that their sex life is boring and run-of-the-mill. They also report that they find themselves comparing their memories of sex in the past, with current, sometimes less exciting, sex lives. These feelings can come to the surface long before teenagers have sex lives of their own, and may be linked to the physical development that is evident in puberty.

Coping with teenagers

- Teenagers actually *need* to see their parents as being in the wrong! This may seem a flippant remark, but behind it lies an important insight. If children are made to do things their parents' way at every turn, they will never develop their own personalities or confidence. Teenagers need to know where you stand on any given issue, because they need a boundary to hit against. In arguing against a certain rule, they gradually begin to form their own rules, and eventually standards of behaviour. This is not to say that you should abandon all hope of making them come home on time! You may find that teenagers need the 'sound and the fury' of opposition more than the opposition itself.

- As with younger children, a united front is important when helping teenagers. Although they may push the limits of your personal codes, you need to support one another. This may be true even if you doubt the wisdom of your partner's decision. You can always discuss your opposition when you are alone – and avoid feeling split between your teenager's demands and your own feelings. It makes better sense to pre-empt some difficulties by thinking through together what may be the 'sticking' points for both of you.

- Some of your beliefs about how your teenager should behave will come from your own upbringing, so tell your partner about yourself and what was expected of you when in your teens. Don't attempt this in the middle of a heated debate with your son or daughter – i.e. 'When I was 16 I wasn't allowed to go to all-night parties, so he's not going to either'. You will only raise the temperature even further. Instead, explain why you feel you agree (or disagree) with your own upbringing at a time when you and your partner both feel able to talk easily. Try to assess why you feel as you do:

  1 Is it blind adherence to a set of rules that may not apply now you have your own family?

  2 Are you worried about your own parent's disapproval if you change a family rule with your children?

  3 Do you want your child to have more freedom (or less) than you had?

  4 Are you sometimes tempted to side with your child to score points

against your partner – perhaps to 'punish' your partner for hurts in
the past?

5   *Adult children*

It is an old adage, but you are a parent all your life, and this can be a
source of joy and pain at one and the same time. Many couples look
forward to the increase in time together once children have left home,
but others dread the change in role that being without children brings. I
often see couples who have had relationship problems masked by
having children to care for. Once the children have left, cracks in the
relationship are more easily perceived, and there is more time to
contemplate what might have been covered over by caring for
children. In fact, there is a slight rise in the divorce statistics in middle
age, and this is often due to the 'empty nest syndrome'. Both partners
can feel a change in role, and this can be particularly acute if children
have been a focus for feelings of self-esteem. It may be hard to admit,
but if your child does well at school, or in a job, or even finds a good
partner, you may bask in the reflected glory. If they are no longer
around every day, you may experience a sense of futility and a loss of
self-worth.

You may also struggle with 'letting go' of your child. As they
establish their own lives, the loss of control over offspring can have a
knock-on effect with a partner. You could notice that you argue more,
or find it hard to discuss your feelings in depth. In a way, you are
grieving, even though your child is still living. This is a natural feeling,
and it is right that you should feel sad at this turning point in life, but
your partner needs to know how you are feeling. Tell him or her about
your thoughts and emotions rather than trying to hide your feelings.

There are, of course, many compensations for children growing up:
you may become a grandparent, or enjoy watching your son or
daughter build a career. If your adult children remain living with you,
though, you need to maintain privacy for yourself, so that your own
relationship is not squeezed out by their lives.

Your relationship when children leave home

- Use the space you have to rediscover elements of your relationship
  that you thought were dead. For instance, what did you enjoy when
  you first met? You may not be able to do exactly the same sort of
  activity, but you could consider something similar. Look around for
  clubs or classes that offer a chance to re-explore these hidden
  pleasures – whether it be painting or motorbiking.
- Many couples tell me that this time can be stressful because they are

not used to spending time with just each other. Make time for yourself as an individual, and try to value this space in your life. It might seem an easy solution to look to your partner to supply the missing boost to your self-esteem, but if you 'feed' from the relationship in this way, your partner may soon feel exhausted at trying to keep you afloat.

- If your family continues to live with you as they grow older, it is vital that you keep a real sense of yourselves as a couple. Lay down rules for the family, and treat them as responsible adults! If you go on doing all their washing and cooking, they may continue to expect this long after they are capable of doing it for themselves. Try to give yourself time to be together. Reinvest in your couple relationship by doing again some of the things you used to enjoy.

Deciding not to have children, or when you find you can't

Many people assume they will be able to have children, and invest time and effort in ensuring the woman does not become pregnant, so discovering you cannot have a baby can be devastating news. Indeed, you may have got together in the first place on the unspoken agreement that you will have a family, so that finding you are unable to have a child may fundamentally change your relationship. It is also likely that you will experience swings of emotion – from feeling you can cope, to great sadness. You may discover that only one of you has fertility problems, so that this partner feels guilty and miserable, while the other may feel tempted to blame them for causing the problem.

Case history
Bridget and Ray met at their local church, and married after a year of getting to know each other. As they planned for the wedding, they talked about what they wanted from their marriage. They were helped in this by the marriage preparation groups that their minister held at the church. They both wanted a family and, as they were in their mid-thirties, decided to start trying for a baby as quickly as possible. When 18 months had passed and Bridget had not conceived, they went to their GP. She referred them for tests at the local hospital, and eventually they found that Ray had a very low sperm count – so low that the chances of them conceiving a child were almost nil. They were offered help in discussing other options in conceiving a child, such as using donated sperm.

41

They were unprepared for how the discovery affected their relationship. Bridget felt depressed and weepy, while Ray felt he had let Bridget down. They sought the help of their minister to discuss their feelings, and slowly realized that they were grieving for the dream of having their own child that they had nourished since falling in love. It took some months before they felt able to look at the options now open to them, but were strengthened by talking through the changes of expectation they had experienced.

Coping with childlessness when you want children

- Make a list of all the positive points about your relationship, and look at how different you life might be without children. Of course, more leisure time or money cannot compensate for the pain of not having a child when you really want one, but your relationship is still worthwhile. In fact, you need each other more than ever for support and encouragement.
- You may encounter sexual difficulties, as sex may seem empty and meaningless, especially if you have been trying to conceive a child for some time. You may find it helpful to put sex on hold for a while when you discover you have fertility problems, and spend some time just cuddling and caressing instead. Then you can rebuild your sex life knowing it may take a different form if you decide to have fertility treatment, or don't ultimately have children.
- Think about your options if you discover you are infertile. Talk to your GP, and gather as much information as possible about alternatives. Your local infertility group may be able to support you at this time.

Making a positive decision not to have children

Many couples tell me that the problems involved in deciding not to have a child are much less to do with their own decision than the pressure they experience from others. Although expectations are changing, society still seems to expect a couple to have children. (Many marriage ceremonies specifically mention childbearing as part of marriage.) If you decide not to have children, you may have to weather the curiosity or tactlessness of those who think you should have had a family.

Having a successful childless relationship

- Carefully talk through the reasons why you have decided not to have children. Make a list of how you feel now, how you might feel in a year, five years or ten years (or any length of time that seems helpful to you). Include practical issues (such as finance) or emotional reasons (such as feeling afraid of childbirth). Talk about how it felt to look ahead, as this might help if you have to deal with other people asking why you haven't had a baby, especially members of your family.

- Remember, this is *your* relationship – not your parents' or friends' relationship. Don't feel pressurized into having a child because everybody else thinks it is a good idea.
- Don't forget to maintain your loving relationship by keeping alive all the good things you enjoy about each other. You will have a different lifestyle to friends who have children, but it could be creative in a way that those who have a family miss out on.

Having children can change a relationship in a way that combines great joy with much pressure. It may cause you to reassess the way you see each other, or even the reason you got together in the first place. However, children can help a couple to grow in understanding and care in a way that can be enormously enriching for all. If the changes that children bring can be successfully negotiated, many couples feel their relationship is strengthened by becoming a parent. However, to be childless (either by choice or misfortune) does not mean your relationship is not valuable. The love that drew you together, and that you have helped to nurture throughout your relationship, is just as important as the love that parents may give a child.

As with all crunch points, you can use the 'helpful' and 'unhelpful' responses to help you develop effective ways of keeping your relationship secure and fulfilling throughout the transition from couple to family.

4

Dealing with Second Relationships, and Learning to Be a Step-parent

Entering a second relationship after the breakdown of a partnership can be both exciting and frightening. Some people attempt to form new relationships very quickly after the end of a difficult relationship, and there are several reasons why people do this. Usually these reasons are connected to feelings of loss of self-worth, and a desire to escape from the loneliness that a person may feel if they are on their own after living with others.

In seeking a new relationship quickly, most people are trying to rebuild shattered images of their own attractiveness. In other words, if someone else can find you attractive then you can deny the pain of rejection, and the possible feeling that your ex-partner must have found you unattractive. Although this is a very natural desire, it can be dangerous to rush into a new relationship. Because you will not have had time to sort out your feelings towards your ex-partner, or understand your own responsibilities in the breakdown, you may take your confused emotions with you into the new relationship. This is rather like starting off on a new journey with a suitcase still full of the dirty washing you had from the last journey. In order to start afresh, you need to unpack your suitcase and sort out what you need to take with you, and what you can leave behind. Starting a new relationship when you are still reeling from the impact of the loss of the last one is the emotional equivalent of carrying a 'suitcase' of unsorted feelings and thoughts with you before you have really understood what you want and need from a new relationship. Chapter 9 deals with this area in greater detail, and you could also re-read Chapter 2, which will help you understand more about starting new relationships.

If you have come through an unhappy relationship, and regained your equilibrium, finding happiness with a new partner after a previously unhappy relationship can help you to feel that life is really worth living again. Couples often tell me in counselling that they feared they would never fall in love again after they had been through the grief of a separation or divorce. However, the pleasure of finding love again can be muted by dealing with the complexities of yours and your partner's children from the previous relationship. *You* may have fallen in love, but your children have not. It is not unusual for parents to imagine they will be able to put two lots of children together, and things will be problem-free. This is perhaps due to the stage that the relationship is passing through (see Chapter 2), and a belief that 'love will find a way'.

The way in which you respond to your new partner's children may match the cycle that relationships pass through. At first, you may go out of your way to be thoughtful and kind, and want to see only good in your partner's children. You may then enter a phase where you feel acutely jealous or resentful of them, and find coping with them as part of the relationship almost impossible. Some second partnerships founder at this stage because the weight of trying to build a relationship is too hard to handle in the face of these explosive feelings. However, relationships that tackle the issues around children in second relationships can be rewarded by feeling that the partnership is stronger for having faced some difficult times and come through.

Second and subsequent relationships –
helping children cope

Your own children

- You may feel it is important to protect your children from knowing about your social life, and feel even more protective once you begin going out with someone new. In some senses, this is true, but your children do need to know what is happening. If you suddenly spring a new partner on them, they may feel shocked and angry, and much less inclined to welcome them to the family. Explain that you are socializing more, and gradually introduce the idea that you will be mixing with different friends. If you make new partnerships you will need time to assess whether they will be ongoing, or short lived. Be wary of introducing new 'friend' after new 'friend', as your children may start to build a relationship with your new partner, only to have it dashed again. This experience will mimic the pain of the separation that has gone before, and harm your relationship with them.

- Because you have been hurt by your partnership split, you may want to blame your partner for all the problems in the relationship. It is dangerous to do this, on two counts. First, your children are biologically 50 per cent of both of you. If you run down their mother or father, your children themselves may feel unconsciously put down by you. Second, if you make a new partnership, your children may struggle to trust your new partner because they will remember your seeming love towards their mother or father, followed by your bitter feelings towards your ex-partner after the split. They may wonder if trying to build a relationship with someone new is worth the bother if you are going to behave in a similar way again. I am not suggesting you shouldn't feel angry or betrayed after a relationship breakdown, but you do need to examine your personal responsibilities for the breakdown, rather than just lashing out at your partner.

Your partner's children

- Accept that you will have to build a relationship with your partner's children. They are likely to feel confused by seeing a new person in their mother's or father's life, and may see you as a threat to the attention their parent gives them. Go in gently, and meet the children gradually, rather than in intensive bursts of contact. At first, it might be helpful to meet on neutral ground – such as a park or cinema trip. Allow the children to approach you, and answer their questions truthfully – but in a way that is appropriate to their age.
- Don't attempt to buy their affection. They are likely to see through this, and to feel cheapened by your approach.
- Accept your own feelings about sharing your partner. You may go through times when you find it hard to share your partner, especially if this is time that is precious to you both. If you deny these feelings to yourself, or feel guilty about them, you run the risk of suppressing the reality of your emotions – and this will make them much harder to live with. You will also understand your partner's children more readily, as they are likely to feel just as you do.
- Don't be rude or derogatory about the children's other parent. It can be easy to fall into this trap, particularly if your partner tells you about his or her previous partner's shortcomings. You could end up being dragged into feeling you have to compete with the other parent for the children's affections. It is important to acknowledge that you can never be the same as their real mother or father, but you might nevertheless have worthwhile contributions to make. You have a different insight and help to offer that will complement the children's natural parents, rather than compete with them.

Building a relationship with both sets of children

The early stages of a relationship can be hard to handle with children around, but making a commitment together (such as living together or getting married) when there are children will require sensitive handling from both of you. Some couples have told me that blending their families together was the hardest task they had to undertake in their relationship, even though their commitment to each other was not in doubt. Each family has its own set of networks, rather like a spider's web. Imagine laying one spider's web over another, and you will have some idea of the many interconnections that could be made in two families being put together. To some extent this is inevitable, and you might be able to use some 'reframing' (see Chapter 2) skills to celebrate the good aspects of this. For instance, older children can help younger ones, or share abilities – like teaching football, or how to cope with a bully at school. But there are headaches, and the 'spider's web' can also produce jealousy, rivalry and sadness. Use the headings in this chapter to help you.

Case history
Jackie and Benjamin married after knowing each other for two years. Jackie had been widowed for 18 months before meeting Benjamin, and Benjamin had been in a long-term relationship which had broken up ten months earlier. He had a young daughter by that relationship, whom he looked after. Jackie had three children, two girls and a boy, the eldest of whom was 14. They had had two holidays together as a family unit prior to the marriage, and Jackie and Benjamin had been encouraged by the friendliness the children showed to each other. Benjamin's daughter and Jackie's youngest daughter had to share a room in their new home, and this was where problems began. Jessica, Jackie's daughter, began to tease Benjamin's daughter, Michelle. Benjamin blamed Jessica for annoying Michelle, while Jackie felt that Michelle should stop upsetting Jessica.

Eventually, Jackie and Benjamin began arguing over the problem. They felt very strongly about the issue, particularly as they couldn't see an easy alternative to the two girls sharing. Both wanted the other to deal with the issue by sorting out their own child. The situation continued for some weeks, with neither prepared to give way. The children were confused, and this made things worse because Michelle and Jessica fought even more. Eventually Benjamin threatened to leave the marriage. This profoundly shocked Jackie who felt the old pain of possible loss attack her once again. She knew how much she loved Benjamin, and made a last-ditch attempt to sort the problem out.

After talking together, Benjamin and Jackie offered the two girls a system of rewards if they could stop teasing and annoying each other. For every day that the girls got along together, they collected stars on a chart. When enough stars had been saved, they could have a small treat – such as a trip to the local swimming pool or a visit to the nearby animal park. Although it took time, the girls settled down together, with only minor skirmishes occasionally, and Benjamin and Jackie felt much less pressurized. They also discovered they could successfully work together to solve a difficulty. Both had been surprised at the depth of their emotions, but saw the experience as part of their growing relationship.

Two families into one

- Acknowledge that creating a happy family is going to require a conscious effort, and will probably take some time. You will make mistakes, but you can reassess and change your mind to suit changing circumstances. As in bringing up all children, you need to talk through how you might handle difficult situations. Use your imagination to picture different scenarios. Some common ones might include:

  1 One set of children is fighting with the other. How could you resolve this situation with fairness? Could you feel biased and, if you do, how could you both deal with this?

  2 Two of your children need to share a room. What issues are likely to surface, and is there anything you could do to help overcome any possible problems? (See case history above.)

  3 Your partner's ex is giving their child expensive gifts. Your children react angrily, and want to share the new toys. Would you both allow this? Or would you feel irritated, but feel unable to take action?

  There are lots of scenarios that will be personal to you, but talking and planning will often take the sting out of painful decisions. You could also include your children in this planning, so that they feel some sense of control in what may feel like a situation in which they are powerless.

- Hang on to your feeling of commitment to one another. At times it may feel as if the children rule your life – especially if you have to be at home every weekend to allow them to stay on access visits. Make sure you have some time to be together as a couple, and enjoy those things that initially brought you together.

In some ways, a new family with step-children is very much like having a baby. You need to put in intensive work and attention in the early stages, while the changed relationships are gelling. As with a new baby, the family will slowly find its feet, and you may eventually feel able to trust all the family members to cope with their extended relationships. If you force a new family to walk before it can crawl, you will feel added pressure. In this situation, the tentative structure you have all built could break down, and you will wonder if you can ever make your step-family a good one.

Dealing with step-children, or introducing your own chldren to a new partner, can feel hazardous. However, you may also experience the creative pleasure of making a new family, and a new chance to love. Many couples building a new relationship together unconsciously use reassessment and 'reframing' skills (see Chapter 1) in order to turn difficult situations into better ones. If a loved parent has died, a new partner for Mother or Father can mean another chance to feel love and security. A successful relationship after the breakdown of a previous one can act as a role model for children to see that loving relationships *are* possible, even if there has been difficulty and stress in the past. This is also true for the adults involved, who can have old hurts healed by finding a loving partner after the unhappiness of separation, divorce or death.

5
Money Management

I see many couples who tell me they argue about money. Sometimes, these arguments are repeated, with the same themes being recycled over and over again. At other times, arguments develop because of a crisis in the couple's financial affairs – debt or job loss can trigger such rows. It might seem as if money should be an area in a relationship that can remain untouched by emotion, and be easily dealt with logically and simply. In truth, the manner in which couples handle money can be a powerful symbol of the way they feel towards one another. The way finance is managed can be an accurate reflection of the way the couple talk to each other, manage childcare, or make love.

Money can also be the last taboo in a relationship. A couple may be able to talk openly about many subjects, but stumble over organizing their money. This may be because money can be 'forgotten' about in a way that communication or sex cannot be. Bills can be pushed into drawers, banks avoided, or credit cards over-used. This leaves the potential for money worries to be consistently overlooked, or dealt with in a hurry and with little planning. As with the other areas we have already discussed, the need to remain open to change is important. You may have to cope with fluctuations in income, or anxiety about lack of money as your relationship progresses, and this will require you to change and adapt.

The power of money – what it means in your relationship

In many relationships, the person who holds the cheque book can wield great power in a partnership. From the weekly shop to the annual holiday, the cash controller can have the power of veto over almost all that their family does. This control may initially come about because the person who earns the money dictates how it is used; or it may be connected to traditional beliefs about who should have a say in the spending of money. These beliefs may be cultural expectations, religious ideals or reflect what happened in the family in which the partners grew up. Many couples successfully negotiate spending and saving, but for others it can be a source of great conflict. It can also mirror unresolved anger, revenge or lack of trust.

Case history
Colin and Rita had been married for ten years, with two daughters, when Colin admitted to an affair: he had been seeing a work

colleague for some months. He told Rita he had thought of leaving her to live with a woman, but had decided to end the affair and stay with Rita. Rita was devastated. She had had no inkling that Colin had been seeing anyone else, and felt angry and miserable at his admission. She also felt guilty at wanting to punish Colin, especially as he told her it was their daughters' welfare that had eventually swayed his decision. Rita felt glad he had chosen to stay, mainly for her daughter's sake, but they never dealt with the deep feelings his affair left them both with. Instead, they tried to get on with their lives as best they could.

Rita had a part-time job as a shop assistant, and had always saved her wages to put towards items in the home. She had also used them to buy small things that she knew Colin liked, such as an occasional bottle of whisky. Colin had grown used to this arrangement, and had often spent his money trusting that Rita could bail them out if a new carpet or set of curtains was needed. Now Rita started to buy herself things with the money she earned; she also secretly opened a building society account, and starting putting money aside. Rita was not sure why this suddenly seemed important, but saw it as 'saving for a rainy day'.

After a while, Colin discovered a problem concerning the family car; the garage told him it would be expensive to repair. Colin knew his own finances would be stretched so he asked Rita to contribute to the bill. Rita refused, saying she had no spare cash. She felt uncomfortable about not telling Colin about her private savings, but also felt a sense of justice that she had secrets he knew nothing about. In some ways, it felt like 'getting Colin back' for the pain he had caused her.

Rita used her money to express her feelings. She had quashed her emotions over Colin's affair, but could not escape feeling hurt at a deeper level. In deciding to open her secret account, and spend more on herself, she was showing what she really felt. She did not trust Colin, although he appeared to want to be part of the family again. In a sense, she kept part of herself 'hidden', feeling that this was a part that could not be hurt if Colin betrayed her again. Colin also felt relieved that Rita did not seem to be badly affected by the affair. In using his money as he had always done, Colin showed both his difficulty in discussing what had happened and his need to 'go on as normal'. This semblance of normality lulled him into a false sense of security, so that when the car needed fixing, both of them eventually faced the anger that stemmed from the affair via the issue of the car repair.

The use of money to express feelings that cannot be spoken is common in couple relationships, and it can be even more complex if the couple have financial responsibilities to former partners and children. Unspoken resentments and jealousies can often be acted out in disagreements about how much ex-partners are paid, and issues about how money is paid or who takes responsibility for payment can be dragged into already complex situations. It is not unusual for new partners to find themselves sorting out financial arrangements for their partner because their partner wants to avoid the discomfort of dealing with these problems. (These types of problems are linked to the 'denial' and 'avoidance' behaviour I discussed in Chapter 1.) Sometimes money can be used as a tool of control in a relationship, and I have counselled women whose partners forced them to explain how they spent every penny, or who kept such a tight hold on money that women ended up trading sexual favours for housekeeping money. These examples are extremes, but they do illustrate the power that money may have in a relationship.

It is interesting to note that couples who live together are often more able to divide money up in an equal way, but once married they may revert to more traditional patterns, where the man is seen as the 'breadwinner' and the woman as the 'homemaker'. This can bring its own sense of tension as the couple begin to see themselves moving from independent people with a willingness to live together to a committed couple who are more dependent on one another. In these circumstances, money can be seen as a 'hot issue'.

How to avoid money-related problems

- As with all potentially difficult areas, openness and a willingness to engage with the issue will go a long way towards defusing worries. Together, draw up a list of all the things you are likely to spend money on – from the frivolous to the vital. Decide which ones you both agree on as being indispensable (from a loaf of bread to paying the electricity bill), then others that are on the border line (like newspapers or cinema trips), and finally those that are only ever likely to be rare treats. Obviously, your most important items will vary according to your need. (If you were a journalist, then reading newspapers might be very important to you!) You may find there are areas over which you disagree. Sometimes leisure pursuits fall into this area, so you will need to negotiate where these fall in the list. Making these decisions may seem strange, especially if you have been together some time and taken a lot for granted, but you should find it helpful in clarifying areas you have both avoided talking about.

- Use your lists to help you further. As you look at what you spend money on, think about *how* you spend the money. In other words, do you use credit cards, cash from wall dispensers or cheques? Maybe you have a wage packet and divide the cash up according to your needs. However you do it, is it working? Credit cards can be beneficial in spreading payment, but not if they are constantly over the limit or in debt. Do you manage to keep track of spending each month? One of the problems in coping with shared money is that there are bound to be times when one of you needs to buy something without the other knowing. Discuss whether you could improve your recording of spending. You might find it helpful to keep a book in which you both enter cash in or out, with both of you having a regular time to review this. (Some home computers also have excellent programmes for ordering household expenses.)
- If you hit serious financial problems, seek help quickly. Not only will your financial posisition deteriorate if you delay, but your relationship could be badly damaged by rows about who ignored that final warning on the bill. Talk to the people you owe money to. Most large companies have help available for this sort of situation, and could assist you in spreading the payments more evenly.
- Make sure that you claim all the benefits you are entitled to – a staggering amount of benefit money goes unclaimed each year. Do not feel embarrassed about needing this kind of help – it could make all the difference to your family. Voluntary agencies (such as the Citizens' Advice Bureaux) also help with practical financial planning and advice.
- Try using the 'reframing' skills I outlined in Chapter 1 to help you deal with the impact of money worries. Instead of saying 'we can't afford a foreign holiday this year', think about what you might be able to enjoy. Make the most of what you have, instead of feeling miserable because you cannot have something different! Some couples do live like this – suspending their life until they can have a new car, a holiday, a bigger house, or whatever. In doing this they fail to enjoy what they actually have in their hands, and may never feel satisfied. This can lead to great stress in a relationship, for a couple could end up feeling their whole relationship doesn't come up to scratch. They may separate, or perhaps spend years criticizing each other in a way that eventually undermines both sets of self-esteem.

When both of you earn a living

The stereotype of coupledom – where the man earns the wage and woman stays at home – is fading fast. Since the Second World War, women have begun (rightfully) to claim equality with men in all areas of life, and especially in the workplace. This is a moral right for women, but it does not change the fact that it leaves those forming new relationships, or those already in committed relationships, struggling to create new ways of managing this change. Some of the difficulties couples tell me about are connected to attempting to balance their parents' style of relating to their own present need. This can lead to complications, because many couples come from families where parents have operated in a traditional way. The couple may understand with their *head* that they need to tackle the issues about both partners working, but react and feel with their *heart*, which may still be sending messages about how their parents saw things. This is slowly changing as more and more families structure their family life with greater diversity, but it is still a source of conflict for many of the couples I counsel.

Case history

Zoe and Rob first met through work. They both worked in computing, and had done well in their careers. After a while Zoe moved from her family home into Rob's flat; both felt pleased that they had found someone who understood their work. They also shared an enjoyment of walking and swimming, and felt that their relationship had a worthwhile future. However, Rob began to feel resentment of Zoe's attitude towards sharing the costs of the flat. Rob felt he paid for the rent and other bills, while Zoe often pleaded lack of cash or bought items for their home that he thought were wasteful. They had never sorted out who would pay for what – for this had seemed unromantic at the start of the relationship. They started to argue, and these arguments were often followed by long silences between them, where nothing seemed to get settled. Zoe felt her money was hers, and that Rob shouldn't expect her to give to the flat. After all, she reasoned, he had lived in it without her. Rob felt Zoe should split the costs now that they were living together.

Zoe came from a family that had a traditional approach to families. Zoe's father had been the 'breadwinner', and supported the family financially. Her mother had worked, but never put her salary towards practical needs in the home. By comparison, Rob's mother and father had split up when he was small, and his mother had brought him up alone. His mother had encouraged him to be practical about money, and he was used to dealing with cash in an orderly way. Zoe and Rob eventually managed to stop fighting and sort out their financial problems, but only after several months of wrangling.

Managing money together

As with Zoe and Rob, once you have been independent, sharing income can come as a shock to the system. You may start out together hoping that managing your money ad hoc will be sufficient. These feelings can be further complicated by how you set up your relationship. For instance, if one of you moves into the other's flat or house, you may develop a split in who pays rent or mortgage, and who pays other bills. This can seem all right for a short time, but can lead to feelings of inequality and resentment.

Points to bear in mind

1 When you decide to form a committed relationship and move in together, talk over how money will be handled. Do this as soon as possible, before a precedent is set by default. You may need the help of a local solicitor in matters of mortgage payments or rent arrangements.
2 If your partner withholds money without your knowledge, then it may suggest that he or she is not as committed to the relationship as you are. Alternatively, spending a great deal on your new partner, or paying all bills, may indicate you are hungry for a relationship and prepared to do almost everything to secure it. Never give a comparatively new partner a lot of money, or agree to payments you do not fully understand. It can be tempting to trust someone in this way if they pay you a lot of attention, but you could lose your money and your heart.
3 Talk over what you might do if financial trouble hits you. Discuss savings and day-to-day expenses, and if any of these would need changing. Of course, you cannot discuss details because the actual situation will be unknown to either of you, but you will both feel prepared in facing a tricky financial situation if you have this kind of rehearsal.

Redundancy and unemployment

Losing a job can be a devastating experience and although your redundancy may have been brought about through problems your employer is having, it can still feel like a personal rejection. It is common to feel as if you did something wrong, and to feel angry or depressed. These feelings are bad enough if you are coping with them alone, but they can have an enormous impact on a couple relationship.

Case history
Nazim and Gita had been married for ten years when Nazim was made redundant. They owned their own house, and depended on Nazim's wages to support them. At first Nazim thought he would find other employment, but as the weeks and months went by, he remained unemployed. They managed on a small redundancy payment for a while, and then Nazim claimed unemployment benefit. Financially, they kept afloat; but Gita became more and more worried about Nazim's behaviour. He became very withdrawn, and sometimes sat and said nothing for hours on end. He began to get up later and later, and stopped scanning the newspapers for jobs. Their family helped by calling round to support them, but Gita's mother told Gita she felt Nazim was getting worse rather than better.

Nazim was suffering from a rock-bottom sense of self-esteem. He felt he had failed Gita, and could not see how he was going to recover his self-worth. Nazim's work had given him a role, and helped define his own view of himself. Eventually, Nazim came out of the hole he found himself in after losing his job, but it took a long time for him to recover his self-worth – and he only really felt back to normal when he found work after 18 months of trying. Even then, he felt worried in case the job disappeared, as it had done before.

Coping with redundancy

- If you are made redundant, tell your partner as soon as you can. Some people keep the job loss a secret, and even pretend to go to work as normal. This is a form of avoidance or denial, for you are really trying to tell yourself it has not happened. It is better to face the truth than risk your partner feeling you couldn't trust them, or breaking their trust in you.
- Make sure your place of work follows the correct procedure for redundancy, according to your length of service and job. If you belong to a union, they can advise you on this. If not, the Citizens' Advice Bureaux can help you decide if you have been treated fairly.
- Allow yourself to feel sad, angry, confused or let down. You may even feel a sense of relief if you have watched others lose their jobs in your organization, and wondered if your turn was coming. It is not

uncommon for someone to become 'stuck' with a particular way of coping with redundancy. You may find yourself constantly eaten up with anger, so depressed that you cry all the time, or feel emotionally numb and uncommunicative. All of these can be hard to deal with in a partnership, and can cause both of you to feel exhausted simply coping on a day-to-day basis. Consider counselling if you feel you are not coping with normal life.

- Although it may seem extremely difficult, you may be able to 'reframe' your job loss in a more positive way. Losing your job could enable you to make a change in the type of work you want to do. You could perhaps re-train in another career, or use skills you already possess in order to change your working life. If your partner is working, and could support both of you, you could experiment by taking some time to discover what you really want to do. You could also explore further education, and distance learning courses such as the Open University.

- Maintain a routine if you find yourself at home for a long period. If you stay in bed late or watch television all day, you may lose the impetus to seek work, and your self-esteem will sink lower. Build a routine that gives shape to your day. Eat at regular times, take exercise every day, and keep your mind active by talking to your partner and friends. You could try surprising yourself by reading books that you might never have previously considered, taking a new route to the shops, or listening to a radio station you would not normally listen to. These ideas may sound insignificant in the face of the major trauma of job loss, but they can help you to feel better about yourself. A positive approach can boost your relationship at this time, and help you both to work together. You can then feel supported and cared for at just the moment you need it most.

Handling money problems can seem a daunting task at different stages of your relationship. However, it is possible to feel a sense of achievement when money is handled well within a relationship. It is true that money cannot buy happiness, or love, but it can help you to reach goals that support your life together without stress or anxiety. By taking time to discuss your mutual financial needs, and sharing hopes for the future, you can make money part of your life together, without feeling dominated by worry over how the next bill is going to be paid. Even if a crisis hits, you can gain a lot by working together as a team, and overcoming the common reactions of blaming your partner, or denying that the problem even exists.

6

Coping with Sexual Problems

In an age when sexual imagery is all around us, it can seem surprising to imagine that sex might still be a problem area for couples. Magazines and newspapers are constantly telling us how to succeed in every area of sex, and we have more access to sexually explicit material than any generation before us. And yet many couples still perceive sex as hard to talk about, and an issue that can cause rows, distance and sadness.

The reasons why sex remains a difficult area for many couples lies in the nature of sexual contact itself. To have sex with anyone (whether that person is a committed partner or a more casual partner) means that one person has to let another person inside their normal defences. By defences, I mean the personal emotional distance we keep from people around us, and the way in which we keep certain parts of our lives private. This is even true for prostitutes, who often draw a boundary between themselves and clients by refusing to kiss them.

In a committed, long-term relationship the degree to which you share the deeper side of yourself can be a source of great joy, but can also lay you open to hurt in a profound way. In a loving relationship, you invite uncertainty into your life. You may hope you know from the way your partner behaves and looks that they want the best for you. But if they let you down, they are already inside the most tender part of you, and the emotional damage can be very painful. To have a sexual relationship in the context of a committed relationship can mean that you have a very intimate partnership, so that when a difficulty emerges, it can feel very frightening. It may even seem as if the whole relationship is under threat.

Couples tackle this difficulty in different ways. As I described in Chapter 1, they use the same responses as in other areas of life. They may deny there is any problem at all, and sometimes struggle on for years feeling confused about why their sexual relationship is so unhappy. If couples do this with a sexual problem, they may also use blaming to cope with their feelings. Sometimes they will blame each other, saying things like, 'He's too old to have good erections', or, 'She never responds if I touch her, so I don't bother any more'. Others may avoid dealing with their concerns, and after a first attempt to change, they slip back into the same old sexual routine. They may even say they have tried to change, and failed, and feel there is little point in trying again. Many sexual difficulties have two very familiar common roots, anger and anxiety, and both of these can cause problems.

Anger

Repressed anger can cause couples to avoid sex, or to develop specific problems with certain parts of their sexual behaviour – such as lack of orgasm or premature ejaculation. It can also lead to a loss of desire for any kind of sexual contact, and sometimes any show of affection is cut off.

Case history
Rosie and Mark discovered this when they began to find sex difficult. They had been married for five years when Rosie asked Mark about when they should start a family. They had agreed before they married that they would like children. Rosie felt she was approaching the age when it would be ideal for them to begin trying for a baby. She was amazed when Mark said he felt it was too early to consider a child, and that they couldn't afford it for at least another two years. Rosie tried to explain she felt differently, but Mark seemed to shut out her feelings. Over the coming weeks, Rosie felt more and more resentful towards Mark. She found herself less able to cuddle or kiss him, and sex gradually stopped happening at all. Rosie knew she felt angry about the child issue, but did not make the connection between her anger and her withdrawal from sexual contact. Mark felt puzzled by Rosie's lack of interest in sex. He sensed her anger, and realized he had hurt her over the issue of starting a family, but felt unable to talk about it for fear of causing more problems.

Mark had always privately been more reticent about starting a family than Rosie, and his feelings had come to a head when Rosie raised the subject. Both of them felt unable to tackle the root of the problem, and sex became a casualty of the anger they both felt. However, the withdrawal of loving closeness also acted as a channel – it let Rosie and Mark 'tell' each other how much they were both hurting without talking. Some couples use this form of communication a great deal. Ultimately it is very destructive in any relationship because the real problem never gets settled, only buried. It is a form of avoidance that has long-term consequences.

Dealing with anger in sexual problems

1 If you feel yourself withdrawing from sexual contact, ask yourself whether you have angry feelings over some aspect of your relationship. Angry feelings can simmer for years, so think back to earlier times. Or look at recent events, and consider if there has been anything that you may have felt irritated by and have not been able to share effectively.

2 Consider talking to your partner, or decide if there is a practical way of solving the problem. For instance, you could be waiting for your partner to notice how annoyed you are about the unpaid bills in the drawer. Instead, you could actually pay them yourself, and decide to discuss a more effective way of dealing with finance in the future. Taking action can help to resolve angry feelings, but you need to build on the action by creating a more helpful way of dealing with the problem next time.

3 If you both find yourself in a situation that makes you feel angry, but is hard to tackle, try a physical means of release.

Anger releases

• Pile your bed up with pillows and hit them with a rolled-up newspaper or magazine.

• Try cycling, jogging or any other active sport that allows you to work off angry emotions.

• Keep a pile of old magazines or newspapers, and tear them up before recycling or throwing away.

• Find an isolated spot and scream or shout loudly, or sing loudly in the car as you drive along!

• Write down the things that are annoying you, and then tear up the paper into tiny pieces.

4 Talking about the anger, and what caused it, is probably the best way to resolve the issue for good. However, you should try to stick to the issue – don't drag in every unhappy event over the last few months, or you will end up feeling weighed down by the past. Choose a time when you can both give the problem the attention it deserves. Avoid deep discussion of sexual difficulties in the middle of love-making. You are more likely to argue at this time than solve the problem. Choose a time when you can feel relaxed and free from interruption. You could start by saying something like, 'I'm having trouble responding to sex because . . .' You should also listen to your partner carefully. Angry feelings can blind you to your partner's responses, so try to be aware of this.

Anger can be connected to the stage your relationship has reached at the moment. You may be able to see a pattern of behaviour that will help you to make sense of your feelings, and allow you both to move on. Say something like, 'I feel that whenever you are worried about your job [or whatever is appropriate to your situation], our sex life seems to suffer. I feel more distant from you. I've noticed this is a pattern we seem to repeat. Is there anything we could do to stop the circle?'

Anxiety

Anxiety can cause real unhappiness in a sexual relationship. Most people know what anxiety feels like; it is the kind of feeling you have just before going on stage, visiting the dentist or having an appraisal at work. Usually these feelings fade away when the event that provoked them is over, but they can be present in a rumbling, low-grade way for a longer period of time; this then undermines sexual confidence.

Case history
Bill discovered he felt anxious when he first met Charlotte. Bill had been married for some years, but sadly his wife had died of cancer. He was feeling very alone, and thought he might never experience another close relationship, when he met Charlotte through a friend. They hit it off straight away, and eventually they progressed to a sexual relationship. However, Bill found that he lost his erection when he tried to penetrate Charlotte. Charlotte was understanding, but Bill felt very upset. He had enjoyed a fulfilling sexual relationship with his wife, and saw his new sex life as an expression of Charlotte's importance to him. He was caught in a circle of anxiety that meant each time he tried to keep his erection, and couldn't, it made him more anxious that next time it would happen again, and this increased anxiety caused the erection to fail again.

Bill and Charlotte decided to seek help from a Relate psychosexual therapist (a therapist who offers assistance with a couple's sexual worries, and who has been trained to offer specific help with sexual problems), who helped them to understand that Bill felt afraid to give himself to another woman. The death of his wife had left him wondering if he could take the risk of loving Charlotte, perhaps only to be hurt again in the future. Bill also realized he felt guilty about having sex with Charlotte – as if he were betraying his wife. Together, Bill and Charlotte worked on these problems by talking to the therapist, and doing some tasks at home that built up their mutual confidence.

If you feel anxious during sex, you may feel your anxiety is related to what you are doing at that moment. However, as with Bill, anxious feelings often have their source in places other than the immediate sexual setting. Common sources of anxiety might be:

- Physical or sexual abuse that took place in childhood; these experiences can seriously affect your ability to 'open up' sexually. Abuse seriously damages an individual's ability to trust that others will not also abuse them, so victims keep their defences high, even if they want to love and be loved.
- Other childhood experiences can also affect your ability to respond sexually. If you come from a family who had difficulty in showing you physical affection, or seemed cold and withdrawn towards you, then you may find it hard to express physical affection to your partner. Conversely, this kind of experience can leave you hungry for any kind of affection, and make you vulnerable to being used in some way by another person.
- Other forms of sexual trauma that you have experienced during your life can also have an effect on your sexual response. The most obvious is rape, or other forms of sexual violence. This is not only true for women; men also can be raped. In fact, there is some evidence to suggest that violent sexual assaults towards men are on the increase. The degree to which you are affected will very much depend on how you feel about the experience you had. Some people feel very affected by unwanted sexual touching, while others recover more quickly. Whatever your feelings, they are your *real* feelings. You may feel tempted to minimize your emotions for the sake of your partner, but it is important to explain what you feel. If you find talking about the experience difficult, it can help to talk it through with a counsellor before discussing it with a partner. Men, as well as women, can suffer from sexual difficulties as a result of sexual abuse. A recent report by Relate showed that 13 per cent of the people they saw for psychosexual problems had suffered some kind of sexual trauma – men as well as women.
- Worry over other aspects of your partnership can stop you feeling relaxed during sex. For instance, you may be concerned that your baby will wake up during love-making, or wonder if your teenage daughter will get home from the disco safely. Successful love-making needs you to feel secure, and able to concentrate without

interruption. If you are distracted, sex will feel disappointing and probably dissatisfying.

- If you lack trust in your partner, your anxiety levels are likely to be high. If your partner lies to you, is violent or has let you down in the past, you may feel resistant to sex and find intimacy extremely difficult. For instance, if your partner has had an affair in the past, and you both want to put it behind you, it may still feel like an invisible barrier between you for a long time afterwards.

Dealing with anxiety in sexual problems

1 Some feelings of anxiety over sex are connected to moving from stage 1 to 2 in a relationship (see Chapter 1). It is not uncommon for couples to feel happy about their sex life for a long time, and then for differences to arise. One partner may begin to feel bored, or taken for granted. You may be aware of these emotions, but feel uncertain how to express them. Try asking yourself, 'What is it I am finding hard to say?' Make a list, or even draw pictures of your emotions. Imagine your anxiety as a ton-weight, and think what makes up that weight. For instance, you might fear you are not making love often enough, or that your previously responsive partner is behaving coolly towards you. Now think about ways in which that weight might be lightened. Some good examples of 'anxiety weight lifting' are:

- Talking to your partner. You don't have to have every thought carefully regulated; simply try to explain how you are thinking and feeling, however incomplete.
- Listening to yourself. Anxiety can sometimes cause people to dismiss their own good instincts, and to churn the problem around and around in their head with no solution. When this particular difficulty first emerged, what was the main feeling you experienced? If you can identify your very first response, you may now be able to allow yourself to take the action you feel is necessary.

Case history
For instance, Pippa felt upset because her boyfriend, Joe, had teased her about gaining weight. She had felt hurt and wanted him to apologize, but he didn't do this. For several weeks, Pippa chased her hurt and angry feelings around and around in her head. One day she decided to act on her first thought, and explained how hurt she had been, and then asked Joe for an apology. He was genuinely surprised he had hurt Pippa, and readily apologized. Pippa felt better, and was eventually able to see the incident as unimportant.

- Inform yourself about sex. Many of the couples I see in therapy lack basic knowledge on how their body works, or how they respond to sexual arousal. Read a reputable book on sex, watch a video guide, or find out if your Local Family Planning Clinic could help you learn more.

  However, beware of semi-pornographic material, which could make you feel even more sexually inadequate. Pornography is often full of myths about sexual behaviour – men who are always ready for sex, women who will do any sexual act if asked. From this point alone, it can harm your understanding of sex, especially if you already feel vulnerable. Survivors of sexual abuse have often told me that seeing pornographic images has caused them to have unhappy flashbacks. So if you feel worried about a sexual problem, pornography is unlikely to help, and in fact could harm – even if you don't have moral objections to it.

2 Be specific about what you want to change. Saying you want a 'better sex life' may state the truth, but it will not help either of you to understand what needs changing to remedy the concern. Perhaps you would like your partner to caress you for longer, or you want sex at a different time of day. Try to decide what you really need to feel more satisfied or relaxed, and then agree to try it together.

3 Only deal with what you can deal with! Worry about anything, especially in sex, can happen because people try to tackle everything in one go. You may think you need to change a lot all at once, but this will end up with you feeling overwhelmed by too much change. Aim for small, achievable goals, and take your time. For instance, decide to have a month when you agree a pact of enjoying at least half an hour of stroking, cuddling and touching before attempting actual intercourse, or consider not always going on to intercourse itself, and simply enjoy the cuddling for its own sake.

Common sexual difficulties

Although each couple's sexual problems are unique to them, most sexual concerns fall into common themes. These problems often emerge at times of change in the life of a couple – perhaps after the birth of a child, retirement or illness. It is also important to remember that most couples go through sexual problems, of one form or another, during their life together. These difficulties may resolve themselves as you talk through your problems, or follow the guidelines above. However, long-standing problems that you find return at times of stress may need professional help. Your first port of call should always be your GP, but you can obtain specialist help from Relate (who train experienced couple counsellors to deal with psychosexual problems), or your local Family Planning Clinic.

Loss of sexual desire

Of all the women who seek help from Relate for sexual problems, this is the greatest concern. Some 40 per cent say they have lost interest in sex, and see this as damaging to their overall relationship. Loss of interest in sex is also increasingly reported by men. For both sexes, loss of desire can be a result of tiredness, stress, or simple boredom with sex that has become stuck in a routine. It can also mask other, more specific, problems. It is easy to see how never having an orgasm, or always ejaculating very quickly, might stop someone feeling interested in sex. (I often see one member of a couple who tells me they have gone off sex, only to discover it is because their partner has a sexual problem that they have been afraid to discuss.) Also, as stated earlier, anger and anxiety prevent couples from feeling interested in sex.

Case history

Jason and Pam found this when Jason lost interest in sex. Jason and Pam had both gone to a party with friends, and Jason had seen Pam kissing a friend of his. Pam didn't know that Jason had seen the kiss. They had all had a lot to drink, and when Pam remembered kissing Mark (the friend) the next day, she decided to say nothing to Jason. She told herself it had only been one kiss, and meant very little to her. Meanwhile, Jason had begun to feel angry and hurt. He found himself wondering if Pam was having an affair with Mark, and anxious in case she was going to leave him. As the weeks went by, and neither of them raised the subject, Jason lost interest in love-making. He felt unable to respond to Pam, and Pam felt rejected and uncertain about Jason's feelings (stage 2 – see Chapter 1). She withdrew angrily, with neither of them able to understand why the problem had occurred in the first place.

Dealing with loss of sexual desire

Pam and Jason did not know how to restore their loss of desire, but loss of interest in sex can be helped by following some of these pointers:

1 Sweeping worries under the carpet prevents either of you from

dealing with the difficulty. As with Pam and Jason, a small concern became a much bigger difficulty because neither partner discussed what had happened. In relationship terms, a 'stitch in time' really does 'save nine'.

If you want to discuss anything, especially a sexual worry, do it as soon as you both have time to discuss the issue. If Jason had asked Pam about the kiss, they would have been able to sort out their feelings, and begin to rebuild their confidence in each other. Jason's anxiety stopped him from finding out the truth, but also created a mountain out of a mole hill. Pam's embarrassment at kissing Mark stopped her from telling Jason. She also used self-denial (Chapter 1) to tell herself it didn't really matter.

Try using phrases like:

- 'I've noticed we seem to have stopped making love. I wonder what has stopped us?'
- 'I feel sad [unhappy, concerned, surprised] that we aren't making love very much. What do you feel about it?'
- 'I used to enjoy our love-making, but my interest in sex seems to have declined. I'd like us to talk about why I feel this way.'

2 Consider changing your approach to sex for just a short while. Offer to give your partner a massage, or ask for one for yourself. For example, agree to make love at different times, and in different rooms, for a month.

3 Accept yourself, and your partner, as you are. Many couples I see are dogged by the belief that they will enjoy sex when they are thinner, prettier or richer. Some people qualify this 'waiting game' still further. Women may say they will only enjoy sex when they have thinner thighs or larger breasts. Men may decide sex will be better once they achieve a flatter stomach and more muscular arms. Others blame their loss of desire on their partner, and tell me they will feel sexually turned on when their partner is thinner or cuts their hair. It is true that it is more pleasant to make love to someone who is well groomed, but if you wait until the diet works or you finish painting the house, you could be putting off finding out how enjoyable sex is right now.

5 Don't try to make love if you have hardly touched each other at other times. Many people I listen to tell me that if their partner is barely affectionate most of the time, but demands sex when they feel like it, then they feel used and angry. In this situation, you can see how someone might switch off their sexual response and lose interest in sex.

6 Relax into love-making. Avoid making love last thing at night when

you are both exhausted from work and family. Try bathing or showering first, and spoil yourself with oils or bubble bath. Light candles, or arrange a low, romantic light. If you are a woman, wear something sensuous that makes you feel good about yourself. Men can also enjoy wearing sexy clothes during love play. Try a pair of silky boxer shorts or a soft shirt. Cuddle and kiss before moving on to sex. Fast sex often means unsatisfying sex. Take your time, and explore what you enjoy, and what your partner likes.

Imbalance in sexual desire

This sexual problem is a variation on loss of desire for sex. Many couples accept that there will be times when one of them wants sex more than the other. It is particularly common after childbirth. However, it can happen at any time, and cause great unhappiness for both partners. One couple explained to me that they both felt extremely pressurized – the wife felt she had to ask for sex all the time, and seize any small sign of affection as a signal of sexual interest from her husband, while the husband felt guilty if he didn't make love when asked, but angry that his wife wasn't sensitive to his feelings.

Case history
This was the way that Jack felt. Maggie had been ill with a severe bout of flu and a chest infection, which had kept her off work for several weeks. As she recovered, she felt very tired, and told Jack she didn't want to make love. Jack accepted this because of her illness, but when Maggie returned to work, and still seemed reluctant to have sex, he felt annoyed and confused. When this situation had gone on for several months, they came to see me. Maggie explained that Jack had given up his usual thoughtful approach to love-making, and seemed to be behaving in a way she hardly recognized. He frequently came up behind her when she was washing up, and grabbed her breasts. If she kissed him at all, he put his hands up her skirt. Jack said he felt frustrated, and felt he had to make the most of every chance because Maggie had become so withdrawn. He found Maggie very attractive, and they had previously had a fulfilling love life. As we talked, it became clear that Jack had been very worried when Maggie became ill. His mother had died when he was in his teens, after a long illness. Maggie had always enjoyed good health, and he realized that he had become sexually demanding after the illness partly because he had been afraid he might lose Maggie too.

Understanding this legacy of the past helped them both, but they still needed to rebuild the balance in their sexual life together. Although your sexual imbalance may not fit Jack's and Maggie's imbalance exactly, you could still be helped by some of the ideas they tried out.

Dealing with imbalance in sexual desire

1 Take the tension out of sex by agreeing to stop actual love-making for a while. (Fix a time limit, such as two weeks, or it could drag on for too long and cause arguments.) Instead, put time aside to have sessions when you caress and stroke one another. You could 'book' these sessions, and make sure you stick to the time.

2 If you are the one who doesn't want to make love, then always explain why you don't. Pushing your partner off, or freezing when they touch you, doesn't help them to understand why you feel the way you do. Try saying something like:
   - 'I'm too tired now, but we could have a cuddle instead.'
   - 'When you demand sex, I feel I want to say no because it feels as if you don't understand my needs.'

   Of course, you will need to find your own words to express your feelings.

3 Agree to make love whenever your partner asks if you can't give a positive reason not to. This may seem a strange idea if you already feel pressurized, but sometimes it can help you both to reflect on what stops you from making love in a more balanced way. For instance, you might discover that your partner always asks for sex on the day you work hardest at work, or at the moment you wanted to relax. If this seems true, then you may be able to decide times when sex would be more appropriate to you both.

4 If you are the one who wants sex more than your partner, think about why you need it. At first, you might describe the problem as almost physical, and you may find yourself feeling something like, 'I get so frustrated it almost hurts' or 'I need sex to remain relaxed'. Then try to decide if this is the whole story. Would you like more affection every day, instead of long periods of abstinence with short, intense sexual contact? Is sex *the* way you show affection, or perhaps the way you bind your partner to you? If you are a woman, are you properly aroused when you make love, and do you experience orgasm? If not, is this a source of frustration, or could it be less important if your partner was more demonstrative?

5 Demanding sex, or always resisting sex, are often ways of letting out anger and anxiety. Jack and Maggie's situation demonstrates this perfectly. Jack had old feelings of anxiety brought to the surface by

Maggie's illness, and Maggie had responded by feeling angry but suppressing it. If you experience this kind of imbalance, try to consider whether you may have these two feelings buried somewhere, and talk to your partner about why you are anxious or angry. Use the same kind of statements I suggested in the section on loss of interest in sex, but tailor them to your own emotions.

Other common sexual problems

As a psychosexual therapist and agony aunt, I help people with many different types of sexual problems. However, many common sorts of sexual difficulties fall into distinct areas, and all of these can be helped by seeking professional support. I would always advise someone who thinks they have a sexual problem to see their GP first. The GP will be able to check out any physical causes of your problem, and advise on your nearest therapist if no physical problem seems obvious. Therapists usually work by talking over the problems with you alone, or as a couple (Relate normally works with couples, but may see you alone under special circumstances), and then suggesting 'exercises' to do at home. You should avoid any therapist who suggests actual sex taking place with them there, or who wants to take part in sexual acts themselves. Check out whether the therapist has proper qualifications (contact the British Association of Sexual and Marital Therapists for more information) and is correctly supervised. All working therapists and counsellors should be supervised to ensure they are working with clients according to the British Association of Counselling's Code of Ethics. The following problems are often called 'sexual dysfunctions', and are common to all sorts of people – whether young or old, newly married or in a longer-term relationship.

Male sexual difficulties
Difficulties in achieving an erection
As the title suggests, this has to do with total or partial loss of erection during or preceding love-making. It can also occur during masturbation, or at times when a man may expect to experience an erection – perhaps during a sexy video, or early in the morning as he wakes up. Erectile problems divide into two areas:

- A man who has *never* experienced an erection. This means not even during puberty, or in other relationships than the one he is in. This

69

form of erectile loss is very rare, and can indicate problems connected to traumatic sexual events from the past (such as abuse), or powerful religious taboos. It can also have a physical cause, and should be checked out by your G.P.

- A man who has experienced erections in the past, but finds that they have been lost in the current relationship. It may also cover partial loss of erection, or when the erection fails just as the man is about to penetrate his partner, or once he is inside her vagina. Many men experience this during their sexual lives, and it can be linked to too much alcohol, tiredness or stress. These one-off events are usually acceptable to most couples, but consistent loss of erection can cause much unhappiness. The man may feel as if he isn't a 'real man', and the anxiety of wondering whether he will 'perform' next time actually makes it more likely he will lose the erection, thereby creating a vicious circle. His partner may question whether she is sexy enough for him, and lose her own sense of self-esteem. Couples sometimes come to me for counselling because the woman has accused her partner of having an affair. I may then discover that the reason she believes this is because he can't get an erection with her, and she assumes he must be having sex with someone else. In fact, erectile failure can happen at any point in a relationship, and to any age of man.

If this happens to you . . .
1 Try to relax more, and avoid sex when you are tired or worried.
2 If you suffer from loss of erection, take your mind off worrying about whether you can get an erection by imagining yourself on a warm beach, with the sound of the sea in the background, or a summer meadow by a river (or anywhere you would feel relaxed and sensuous). Imagine making love there, unhurried and at peace. Allow your partner to arouse you, and enter into the feelings. It can be tempting to distance yourself from these feelings because of your anxiety, so allow yourself to really enjoy the touches and caresses of your partner.
3 If your partner loses their erection, never tease them about it. It will not seem funny to them, and requires tact and understanding from you to deal with the situation. Offer reassurance, and suggest spending more time arousing each other. Try to avoid being angry with your partner. Men who lose their erections cannot control the loss by thinking about it, as the root of the problem lies in their unconscious.
4 Try to decide if the problem seems linked to anything else. Have you

suffered a bereavement, or moved house? Or did you have an especially upsetting argument? Did the erection loss take place suddenly, or slowly diminish? If the problem continues, and you choose to seek help, the therapist or doctor may need to know the answers to some of these questions.

Premature ejaculation

Until recently, this was the problem most men presented with at psychosexual therapy (although this has since been overtaken by erectile problems). Basically, premature ejaculation means to ejaculate either before the man can enter his partner, as he enters his partner, or after a very short while of thrusting into his partner. As with erectile problems, many men experience the odd time when they ejaculate too quickly for their own or their partner's satisfaction. Tiredness, or long breaks between acts of sexual intercourse, can cause this problem. If it is more persistent it can undermine an otherwise good sex life. Men may feel as if they are 'trigger happy', and not able to properly 'satisfy' a partner. Premature ejaculation goes against the myth that to be a man means to have strong erections that last for ages, and that a 'real man' controls ejaculating until the woman reaches her climax. Although this is just a myth, premature ejaculation can cause a man to feel he is not 'good enough'. His partner may lose patience, and feel a sense of rejection if her partner 'comes' very quickly, and then refuses to meet her sexual needs.

If this happens to you . . .
1 If you suffer from premature ejaculation, you may be tempted to distract yourself from sexual stimulation by thinking of shopping lists, or all the players in your local football team. On the whole, this is of limited help. It will eventually distract you from enjoying any sexual sensation, and stop you recognizing when you are about to climax. Ask your partner to stimulate you by hand, and ask her to stop when you reach the point of 'coming'. Do this a few times before attempting intercourse. Don't worry if you ejaculate unexpectedly. Eventually, you will become more expert at recognizing the point at which you need to slow down or stop.
2 Do not use any creams or potions advertised in men's magazines to stop you ejaculating too quickly. They can be irritants, and could cause you and your partner a great deal of discomfort.
3 Enjoy arousal and touching for its own sake. Ejaculating is not the only pleasure in sex, so allow yourself to slow down.

Retarded ejaculation

This difficulty is the opposite of premature ejaculation. The man can feel aroused, and have a good erection, but does not ejaculate. Sometimes he will be able to ejaculate in masturbation, or with a partner's stimulation by hand, but not be able to ejaculate inside his partner. Other men do not ejaculate at all. As with all dysfunctions, get this problem checked out by your GP, as it can have physical reasons as well as psychological ones. Often, both partners tell me of frustration, especially if they wish to start a family. The man may wonder if there is something physical 'blocking' his ejaculation, and the woman may feel as if she is not able to stimulate her partner as she would like to. Both can experience a feeling of isolation, and couples often ask me anxiously if anyone else has had this difficulty.

If this happens to you . . .

1 Men who suffer from retarded ejaculation may have trouble focusing on the physical sensations of sexual intimacy. They often report feeling easily distracted, and can be disturbed by noise or the presence of others in the house. Take positive steps to aid privacy by unplugging the phone, and choosing times for love-making that you know will be undisturbed.

2 As with other sexual concerns, relaxation is vital. Try using some of the relaxation tapes available, or ask your GP for information on other forms of relaxation. This can include aromatherapy, massage or special classes for relaxation.

3 Some men who have retarded ejaculation find it difficult to allow sexual images and thoughts to be part of their love-making. Allow your partner to arouse you while you imagine erotic scenes for love-making.

4 If you are able to ejaculate by masturbation, ask your partner to stay with you while you masturbate.

5 Seek help from a therapist, who will have a range of further techniques to aid you.

Female sexual difficulties

Vaginismus

I see many women who are affected by this painful condition. Basically, vaginismus is an involuntary clenching of the muscles in the lower part of the vagina. This muscle spasm happens whenever a woman attempts penetrative sex, and can happen when she tries to put something into her vagina – anything from a finger to a tampon. Some women only become aware of the difficulty when having a cervical smear test done, and find they are unable to allow the examination to take place. While there can be physical reasons for ths problem, it is often caused by psychological difficulties. It is important to have your GP check out any possible physical reasons, as therapy will be less successful if there are underlying physical problems. Women who suffer from this difficulty are often desperately upset at what they see as an 'abnormality' in their sexual response. They may long to be able to have penetrative sex, especially if they want to start a family. Many women say that the more they try to allow penetration, the more difficult it becomes. In other words, the muscle spasm is not under the conscious control of the woman. Sometimes they describe the muscle spasm as if it is a 'block' in the way of the vagina, or they fear they have a 'closed', or especially small, vagina. (This is extremely unlikely.)

In fact, women who suffer from vagismus are often highly sexually responsive, and have often experimented with other ways of satisfying themselves and their partner. They can often orgasm by manual stimulation, and experience pleasure in arousing their partner. Vaginismus can be caused by a variety of background concerns. Sexual ignorance, or coming from a family where sex was never explained, is common in vaginismic women. Sexual trauma can also be a strong reason why women develop vaginismus – events such as rape or childhood sexual abuse. The reasons may seem obvious in this case, since the woman may fear the pain of intercourse, or emotionally defend against anything entering the vagina. This may still be true even if she loves her partner, and wants to have intercourse with him. Sometimes vaginismus can appear after a previously problem-free sexual relationship. This may be as a result of a traumatic happening, such as a difficult childbirth or a hysterectomy.

The partner of a woman suffering from vaginismus may feel a sense of rejection, or even anger, that his partner cannot have intercourse. Some men tell me they feel inadequate, and unskilled as lovers, because they cannot help their partner to 'open up'.

If this happens to you . . .
1 Seek help from your GP. He or she will be able to reassure you, and advise you on the best course of action. Psychosexual therapy is very effective in helping women with vaginismus. Some 80 per cent of women who have sought help from Relate psychosexual therapists have felt that they have experienced improvements in dealing with their vaginismus.
2 Try exploring your own vaginal entrance, and learning more about the way you are made. You could do this while relaxing in the bath.

Don't force yourself, but gently use your fingers to help you feel more confident about touching your vaginal area.

3 If you feel you know little about sex in general, read a good sex manual, and talk about your feelings with your partner.

Dyspareunia

Dyspareunia means painful sex – that is, the woman can allow penetrative sex, but it causes pain. It is very important to have this difficulty checked by a GP, as some dyspareunia is caused by physical problems that can be easily helped. However, a large proportion of the women who I see for dyspareunia often discover it is due to lack of arousal, or lack of accompanying vaginal lubrication. Most women need to be sexually aroused and stimulated in order to allow the vagina to expand, and for their natural lubrication to properly prepare the vagina for intercourse. If this preparation does not take place, then intercourse may well be painful. This can lead to the woman avoiding any sexual contact, and her partner feeling unwanted and isolated.

If this happens to you . . .

1 Try to identify the type of pain you are experiencing. Is it sharp as your partner enters you? Or stinging, aching or on one particular side of the vagina? It is useful to know this, as your GP and therapist will be able to help you more effectively if they know the type of pain you are experiencing.

2 Make sure you build in plenty of arousal time for both of you. Women sometimes need longer arousal times than men, so allow at least half an hour (or whatever seems suitable) of touching and caressing to ensure you are ready for penetration.

3 Help your partner to know what you find arousing by placing your hand over his hand, and guiding his caresses. Let him know what you find pleasurable by telling him. It can be tempting to express yourself in negatives such as 'Don't do that' or 'I wish you'd stop rubbing me so hard'. However, you may find this works against both of you, so use praise and specific guidance instead – saying something like, 'That's lovely – please do it again', or 'I love it when you kiss me there'.

4 Use a preparatory lubricant (such as KY Jelly or Senselle) to help you if you are making love after childbirth, or after a gynaecological operation. (Of course, these lubricants can be used at any time, but are especially helpful after these events.)

4 Painful intercourse can occur at the menopause, and is often related to hormone changes throughout the body. Seek help from your GP,

and consider using some of the hormone treatments available for this difficulty. Alternatively, use the steps above to help both of you readjust.

Orgasmic difficulties

It is easy to imagine that, with all the coverage in women's magazines and the various techniques that they suggest, all women are now easily orgasmic. But there are many women for whom orgasm is still difficult, and who feel that this problem adversely affects their relationship. Sometimes lack of orgasm is linked to a sense of ambivalence about the commitment in the relationship. A woman may subconsciously hold herself 'in check' until she feels more certain about the nature of the relationship. It can occasionally be caused by physical problems, so consult your GP before seeking other forms of help.

Orgasmic difficulties can occur at different stages in a relationship, and for a variety of reasons. The ability to orgasm can be affected by tiredness, illness, stress or other worries in a relationship (such as money problems or concerns about children). If you suffer from this problem, it may be that you have never had an orgasm, or perhaps been able to achieve orgasm through self-stimulation, but not during intercourse or with your partner arousing you. Women often tell me they feel aroused, and close to 'coming', but somehow cannot climax.

If this happens to you . . .

1 Women often make the mistake of expecting their partner to know what arouses them without sharing what it is they enjoy. If you feel you need certain types of arousal to achieve orgasm, tell your partner what you would like.

2 Experiment with touching and caressing yourself. Imagine yourself climaxing, and allow yourself to enjoy the sensations that wash over you.

3 Assess whether you are pushing yourself too hard, and trying to be sexually responsive when you are tired and therefore least able to get the most from sexual contact. Try to arrange love-making for times when you are feeling fresher and more responsive.

4 Are you judging yourself too harshly? Some women I see are able to have orgasms, but feel their orgasm does not match up to the sort of sex they see on television or in films. If *you* feel satisfied, then that is what really matters.

5 Some women who suffer from lack of orgasm do so as a result of the feeling that sex is something they feel ashamed of enjoying. Often

COPING WITH SEXUAL PROBLEMS

these feelings originate from childhood, and come from parents who have given the woman misleading (or no) information about sex. You can combat this by learning about how your sexual response works, and asking a therapist to give you more accurate information.

Sexual problems can feel overwhelming to a couple, but if you seek help, or use the information in this chapter, you will be far better able to cope with these issues. Many people imagine that sex should somehow remain static, and that shifts in a sexual relationship imply there are fundamental problems. It may be that changes in sex, as in other areas of your relationship, are opportunities to explore new facets of your partnership, and could bring you both a new way of viewing your relationship.

7

Dealing with Affairs, and Loss of Trust in Your Partner

During my counselling career I have seen hundreds of couples who have been through the agonizing problem of losing trust in a partner. Loss of trust can be extremely difficult to deal with – *and* to recover from. One couple I saw described this feeling as being like 'taking a hammer to a Wedgwood plate, and then trying to piece it back together'. I feel they expressed exactly what does seem to happen when one (or both) people in a partnership break trust with the other.

If you have been through the stages of growth in a relationship (see Chapter 2), and know each other well, you will have invested a great deal of yourself in one key relationship. In a way, you have put all your eggs in one basket. This will have required courage and perseverance, and a real determination to make things work. That is why it is so painful if your partner lies to you, has an affair, or deceives you in some other way. Acts of deception can seem like an 'accident' and, when viewed from the outside, they do seem to bear some of the hallmarks of accidents. They often seem to burst upon the couple without warning. Many people I see say things like, 'I don't know why I had the affair – I just found myself in bed with him/her'.

Loss of trust in a relationship is often extremely shocking, and can lead to a couple taking snap decisions about the future of their relationship. It can also leave both partners in the couple feeling confused, emotionally numb and wondering what to do next. Just as the couple above described their 'broken plate' feelings, it can seem a daunting task to try to pick up the pieces of your relationship and rebuild the trust you once had.

But viewing affairs, or similar events, as 'accidents' overlooks something very important: nearly all problems over broken trust are preceded by events that might have indicated danger ahead if the couple had been open to understanding the signs early enough. The seeming 'accident' of an affair is rather like the last scene in an Agatha Christie film. In order for the audience to understand why all the characters have been gathered together, they will have needed to follow the twists and turns of the plot, and made their own guesses about who murdered the victim. Similarly, couples may feel as if they have been presented with an impenetrable crisis, but in hindsight they often tell me there were clues to be found well before the 'crunch' hit them.

Case history

Ros and Phillip were like this. When they came for counselling, the first meeting was completely taken up with the awful emotions they were experiencing. Ros admitted an affair she had been involved in for several months, and Phillip described Ros's admission to him as 'a bolt from the blue'. Initially, Ros had told him she was going to leave him with her lover, Simon. She explained she had been seeing Simon for seven months, and wanted to be out of her marriage to Phillip. Simon was married with two small children, and planned to leave his wife. Ros and Phillip had a son aged 2, whom Ros wanted to take with her. Phillip was devastated and begged Ros to stay. Ros agreed to try again, and very reluctantly gave up her relationship with Simon. Phillip felt there had been few problems in their five-year marriage, but Ros said she had been increasingly unhappy (see stage 1, Chapter 1). She felt that Phillip expected too much of her, and seemed afraid to give her personal freedom. Ros said that Phillip wanted to do everything with her, and she couldn't even go shopping without him coming along.

Phillip's mother had died just before their son was born, and this had been a very difficult time for Phillip. Ros felt that when this happened they had stopped talking in an open way, and that Phillip had shut her out from his feelings. Ros increasingly felt that Phillip demanded a lot of emotional closeness from her, but gave little back, and could be cool and distant. Gradually they discovered that what at first had seemed like a sudden happening, had in fact a long history stretching back to the early years of their relationship. Counselling helped them to unravel some of the clues from the past, and they began the long journey towards recovering from the breach of trust they had endured.

Seeing the signs

1 A change in the normal way you relate to each other
Watch out particularly for one partner becoming quieter and more withdrawn than usual. The change may be sudden, or more gradual, but you may notice you feel as if you are constantly 'crossing the wires' and not communicating as freely as you have done (see stage 1, Chapter 1).
2 Increased tension, with more frequent rows that often return to the same problems
You may find you disagree about money management, childcare or

sexual matters. Frequent blaming and avoidance (see Chapter 1) are often strong indicators of the need to get to grips with problem areas in the relationship.

3 'Stonewalling'

By this, I mean partners refusing to listen to each other in any meaningful way. Sometimes 'stonewalling' includes rushing out of the room and slamming doors, or driving off in the car, the moment any attempt to discuss worries begins. Also, couples often tell me they talk over each other, and neither feels listened to.

4 Intuitive feelings that something is not 'right' with the relationship

I would always suggest that intuition needs checking against reality, but sometimes a feeling that just won't go away is an important one. It might be telling you something about your relationship that is worth investigating.

Case history

For instance, Marie felt this way about Gerry, her husband. Marie felt Gerry had been quiet and miserable for some time. They had always had the sort of marriage where they could talk openly, but this stopped when Gerry started a new job. Marie asked Gerry if there were problems at work, but he denied this, and became very defensive when Marie asked him about work. Eventually, she found a letter from a woman Gerry worked with; it was an arrangement to meet her. Marie confronted Gerry, and he told her that the woman had been pursuing him since he started at the new firm. She was above him in the hierarchy, and he was afraid that if he turned her down he would lose his job. Although no affair had taken place, Gerry had lied to Marie because he did not know how she would respond to the problem. Once it was out in the open, both were able to decide a plan of action over what amounted to sexual harassment by the woman at work.

5 A recent crisis or upset in the family

By this, I mean a bereavement, job change or birth of a child. Sometimes these sorts of events cause individuals to question their whole lives, and can lead them to behave in a way that they may not have done before.

Case history

Sue felt like this when she returned to work after losing a baby as a result of a miscarriage. She and Harry had tried for a baby for some years, so that the loss of their much desired child had hit her very hard. She found it hard to talk to Harry about all they had been through – somehow she wanted to spare him her distress when he felt so unhappy himself. She began to confide in a male colleague, and the friendship became an affair. Sue and Harry eventually parted, as the trauma of the affair so soon after the miscarriage caused them to feel daunted at the prospect of rebuilding their relationship.

6 Reaching mid-life, or some other age that is significant to the couple

The 'mid-life crisis' has become an over-used term, often cited when anybody does something unusual in their forties! However, there is still some truth in the idea that more people have affairs at this time. Reaching 40 can seem a milestone for some, and is an age that can seemly particularly tough to handle. It is at this point that a couple may have teenage, or older, children. Having teenagers around can remind the parent of their own youth, and some people find this difficult if they feel they lost out in some way when younger. As the children leave home, parents may experience a loss of role, and reassess who they really are. Grandchildren are yet to arrive, and the sudden feeling of being a couple alone again can be disturbing. Affairs that happen at this point are often connected to a longing to avoid dealing with these changes, or a desire to put the clock back and start again.

How to talk about loss of trust

Affairs, and other problems over loss of trust, are difficult to discuss because they provoke such painful feelings in both partners. The feelings of guilt from the person who has had the affair – and the hurt, anger and, sometimes, the desire for revenge from the other partner – can seem to prevent any chance of understanding what has happened. But if you can talk together in the aftermath of a crisis, it can help you both to deal more effectively with the future:

1 When you first hear, or tell, the news about an affair it will be hard to remain calm and collected. You might experience a feeling of numbness – as if you are divorced from your surroundings. This feeling often accompanies shock of any sort, and will make it hard to hear, or tell, such life-changing news. For this reason, it is important to choose the time at which you tell your partner. Don't blurt it out

during a row, or wait for someone else to tell them. You could begin by saying something like, 'I have something difficult to talk to you about . . .' If you are hearing the news, listen to your partner carefully; let them finish what they need to say. You may want to jump in straight away, but you will be better equipped if you get as full a picture as you can. It is natural to feel angry and let down, so express this if you need to, but avoid becoming aggressive, or rushing out (avoiding). These tactics will prevent you from dealing with in the present what will still need to be sorted out in the long run.

2 If you are telling the news, then be honest. Tell the whole story, and avoid keeping certain parts secret. You may believe it is kinder to be economical with the truth, but you run the risk of causing more hurt in the future if your partner discovers further deception. Answer questions honestly. If you respond to questions by saying, 'You don't need to know that' or 'I don't know', your partner will respond by wondering what you have to hide.

3 If you are hearing the news, then give your partner time to tell you. Don't interrupt, and try to remain as calm as possible.

As time goes by, the effect of the breach of trust will come to the surface. You may find that in the early days you both feel uncertain about what has happened. Alternatively, you may respond instinctively by deciding to split up. The person who has had the affair may move out, or may say they need 'space' to deal with their feelings. This can work against you because any feelings you both need to work through just become delayed if you are away from each other, or crammed into brief meetings that are fraught with tension. Occasionally a break can help to clear the air, but it is much better to try to live through the difficulties if you can.

Recovering from an affair

Recovering from an affair takes a long time. Neither of you will deal with the profound effect of a loss of trust in a few weeks or months. If you do decide to stay together, you will face a tough time.

You may notice all or some of the following:

- *The partner who has not had the affair wants to know exactly where the other partner is, and what they are doing.*
  You can deal with this by keeping promises about what time you will be home, and being trustworthy when you are out. Some

couples I have seen in counselling have arranged to meet ex-lovers secretly to say goodbye, or to try to keep an association alive. The truth is that there is no middle ground in the matter of affairs – they are either over, or still ongoing. Trying to keep some kind of relationship with your ex-lover is nearly always a recipe for disaster, simply because the trust between you and your partner will take much longer to build. Sometimes it is unavoidable if your ex-lover is a member of the family, or other relative. In these cases, try to meet them with your partner if you have to.

- *You feel a need to know all the details of the affair. If you have had the affair, then you may want to tell everything in graphic detail.* This is a natural response, but it does have dangers. You could help yourselves by agreeing a pact about when you talk about the affair, and when you don't. For instance, you might designate an hour a week for questions or discussion, and then try to live more positively the rest of the time. If you ask questions about details of the affair, remember you will have to bear the answer. This sounds strange, but you may just be torturing yourself unnecessarily. Some people deal with this by feeling better once they know every detail, while others find it seems to twist the knife in the wound every time they know more.

  Wanting to admit every detail of the affair at once may be because you are seeking a 'confessional'. This desire to purge yourself of the feelings of guilt may seem helpful, but it is likely that the feelings will still be there, and will return occasionally. It is better not to load your partner in this way, but to answer their questions as honestly as you can, and allow them emotional room to process what you are saying. Confessing may also indicate that you want somehow to pass the responsibility for forgiveness on to your partner, but ultimately you will have to deal with these feelings within yourself.

- *You want to hurt your partner as much as they have hurt you.* Again, a natural response, but, if acted on, can be very unjurious to the relationship. Some couples I have counselled found themselves in 'tit-for-tat' affairs, where the feeling of rejection was so deep that the partner without a lover immediately sought someone to make a relationship with. This action eventually meant that neither trusted the other at all, and often meant the relationship ended. Other instances of revenge include refusing to speak to the partner, withdrawing sex and other expressions of affection, and telling friends and family what s/he has done. It is important that the feelings of anger and betrayal are expressed, and that there should be room for them to be listened to by the partner who has had the affair.

Using your 'pact' time for this can be helpful. Sit facing each other, and agree on half-an-hour each. Take turns to talk, beginning your sentences with 'I feel . . .' Doing this means that you have to think carefully about what you do feel, and also helps you to take responsibility for your feelings. While one of you talks, the other must listen, maintain eye contact, and avoid interrupting. You may both have to be prepared to hear some hard things, but you will only move forward if you can deal with these difficult emotions.

- *You miss the person you had the affair with.*

Except for the most transitory of one-night stands, having an affair means having some kind of relationship with another person that was of importance to you. (And even one-night stands can be important to you if they were particularly exciting or passionate.) You may have crammed all the stages of a relationship into stolen time together, which became much more intense because of this. Lovers can become idealized in the mind's eye because they have not had to face the rough and tumble of everyday life. If your affair was lengthy, you will need to grieve for the person you no longer see. Your partner is likely to find this very hard, and may put pressure on you to dismiss her or him from your mind. Explain that although you have chosen to stay with them, you will need understanding and support to cope. This may seem a tall order for your partner, but sometimes couples find that sharing in this way encourages them to feel closer. It does require both of you to attempt to enter the other's world of feeling, and a sense of commitment.

- *You wonder if the relationship can be saved at all.*

Although you may want to stay together and sort the relationship out, there will be times when it all seems untenable. You are bound to have arguments, but you may also feel there are enough good times to counterbalance these. However, if you find yourselves constantly rowing, or engaging in 'stonewalling' (no. 3 in 'Seeing the signs' above), then it could indicate that the relationship needs expert help. Relationship counselling could help you to decide which direction to take. You could go together, but it could also help you on your own if your partner is unwilling to go with you.

Any violence indicates serious problems. Seek help from your GP, or other health adviser. Sometimes violence emerges when there is a powerful desire to take revenge for the affair, but never assume it will be a one-off event.

All the above measures can help you to identity danger signs, and how to act if an affair has already happened. However, prevention is much better than cure, and there are steps you can take to avoid affairs in the first place.

Preventing affairs

1 Keep thinking and talking about the 'basics' (Chapter 1) in your relationship. If you both *assume* that your partner feels the way they did six months or six years ago about certain issues, then you may gradually drift apart as you both change. It is easy to assume (often wrongly) that your partner still shares your viewpoint if you never check this out. Ask your partner to tell you about their views on your relationship. You can start by saying something simple like, 'When we first got together we thought very similarly about—— [choose your own topic]. Do you still feel the same?' At first sight, this may seem stilted if you are not used to talking in this way, but gradually your own thoughts and emotions will emerge.

2 Try to maintain a balance between work and leisure. Some affairs occur because work takes over one partner's life – or even both partners' lives. Friendships at work can take on much more significance if you spend a long time at your workplace: these friendships may then grow into relationships that eventually become affairs. In other words, the work environment can be like a 'hothouse', making a relationship that probably wouldn't stand up to normal life seem tenable. It may also be difficult for the partner who is left alone a great deal. They may seek affection elsewhere if they find themselves alone, or unconsciously use an affair to draw attention to the situation.

Time spent with your family will also help to prevent stress, and help you to feel closer to your partner. Use the time you have as a couple as effectively as you can by doing things together you enjoy. This can vary from DIY (yes, some people actually enjoy it), to having a drink at the pub.

3 If you have children, then you need to hold a careful balance between caring for them, and caring for your relationship. Some couples give an enormous amount to their children in time and effort. As they grow older, the requirements of children do not diminish, and could even be said to become greater. Many parents describe feeling like unpaid taxi drivers as they ferry younger children to music lessons, cubs and brownies, and sporting clubs, and older children to each other's houses or clubs. Perhaps one of the reasons we invest a lot in our children in this way is to produce a

child whose abilities and aptitudes allow us to bask in their reflected glory. However, we do this at a cost. Couples who invest so much in their children may find they haven't got a relationship left once the children leave home. Your children are important – but if your relationship fails, then they will be far more unhappy than if they missed the odd cub session or night out. Give yourself proper time to be together alone and relaxed. This doesn't mean spending every spare evening with other couples. I often counsel couples who tell me that they do have time together, but actually only see each other in the company of friends. Of course, seeing friends is important, and a network of friends can support your relationship in other ways, but they should come second to the relationship between the two of you. If you find yourself booking up to be with friends all the time, ask yourself if you are avoiding being alone together, and why you are doing this.

4 Physical satisfaction is a vital ingredient in most relationships – and this can range from a hug to full sexual intercourse. Many people find it hard to talk about sex, but it is important to try to do this or you could wonder if your partner still fancies you, or enjoys the sex you are having. For lots of people, the term 'affair' means sex, but, as you have read, sex is often low on the list of attractions to a lover, after other attributes such as friendship and openness. Your sex life will change with the length of your relationship (see Chapter 2), or the stage you have reached in life – from childbirth to retirement. This means you both need to keep assessing what you enjoy, and what your partner enjoys. Ask each other what you like, both during sexual contact and at other times. You could try saying, 'Do you like it when I touch you here?', or take your partner's hand and use it to caress you just the way you would like. You wouldn't dream of eating the same meal every day in exactly the same way, or forcing yourself or your partner to eat something they disliked, and sex is very similar. Find out what could be on the menu, and try it! I'm not suggesting you do something sexual you would hate, but you could negotiate with your partner to try something different. You could also explore other ways of being intimate as a couple – from mutual massage to reading an erotic book together. This could increase your repertoire, and allow you to express your sexual relationship in a wider context.

5 Value yourself. One of the chief causes of affairs is a lack of self-esteem, both by those who have affairs, and their partners. If you lack self-esteem, it can be tempting to respond to the first person who pays you attention, especially if you feel your partner doesn't

value you in the same way. If you lack a sense of self-worth, your partner can pick this up, and then gradually begin to treat you *as if* you were worth less. You can keep self-esteem alive by paying attention to your overall health. Eat sensibly, and drink within safe limits. Try to take some exercise – even walking can be helpful.

Set yourself small achievable goals. For example, you may decide to read the book you've always wanted to read, see your favourite team play, or have a new haircut. Think back to your teens and try to remember if you had any dreams you haven't thought about for years. These may seem unachievable as an adult, but they could translate into something worth having now. You may recall wanting to be a great dancer, or play snooker like an expert, or to sing in a rock 'n' roll band. You could use these dreams to get you along to a beginners' dancing class, or to the snooker hall, or to learn to play the guitar.

6 Think positively about your partner, and tell them the attributes they have that you value. Many couples that I see criticize each other constantly, finding fault with every small thing. One wife criticized her husband for buying blue toilet paper instead of green! She failed to thank him for doing the shopping in the first place. He criticized her for leaving lights on at night when she got up to attend to their small son, but never thanked her for dealing with a crying baby night after night. It may sound banal, but telling your partner you are grateful for their contribution to the relationship can help you both to feel cared for, and raise individual self-esteem. Similarly, telling your partner you love them can be a great self-esteem boost. You may know you love your partner, but never say it. This could leave your partner wondering if you really feel it. You can regard these loving comments as 'packaging' that helps to shield the relationship if a crisis hits. However, unlike packaging, they also form part of the relationship as a whole, and give it a life of its own.

If asked, many couples would say that an affair is one event in a relationship that could not be prepared for or got over, yet the experience of many couples gives the lie to this. In this chapter I have tried to show how you could survive – and, more importantly, avoid – this most dramatic of changes in a relationship. In the next chapter I aim to help you deal with change that seems to come from nowhere, and leaves your relationship feeling under attack.

8

Circumstance Beyond Your Control

In previous chapters we have looked at events that can rock your
relationship, but that can be – at least partly – under your control. In
this chapter I want to discuss the kind of change that is *beyond* your
control. This kind of change can be the most difficult to deal with
because of the strong feelings of helplessness you and your partner can
experience. Other types of change can feel overwhelming, but it is
sometimes possible to make sense of the change by facing your own
responsibilities, and moving through the cycle of change. When
change comes that seems to be out of the blue, it can feel much more
difficult to decide which parts you can make a difference to, and which
you need to let go of.

Case history
Jack and Roger had been married for five years when they
discovered that Jackie was pregnant. They were both delighted, and
the pregnancy went well; Jackie subsequently gave birth to a
healthy daughter, Poppy. However, after a few months, Poppy
developed breathing problems, and seemed to have frequent colds
that prevented her from breathing properly. One night, Poppy
suffered severe breathing difficulties and was admitted to hospital
as an emergency. She was diagnosed as having asthma, and Jackie
and Roger were helped to understand how to give her the
appropriate medication. Jackie and Roger felt they had dealt with
the situation well, but were sad for their little girl. As Poppy grew
older, she had frequent asthma attacks, which were usually worse in
the winter. She often woke in the night, and needed help with her
inhaler. Jackie found it was usually her responsibility to get up to
comfort Poppy, partly because she had given up her job when she
was born, and Roger was still working. He found it hard to get off to
work on time when he had a disturbed night. But as time went by,
Jackie became resentful that the chief burden of coping with
Poppy's asthma seemed to fall on her shoulders and she and Roger
began to argue. Jackie angrily told Roger she felt unsupported, and
Roger countered by saying he felt he did his best, but he had to work
to keep them all.

Jackie eventually decided to take her mother into her confidence,
and explained how difficult it seemed to deal with Poppy's illness –

and Roger's attitude. Jackie's mother had already observed that things seemed strained between her daughter and son-in-law. As they talked, Jackie's mother helped Jackie to realize that she had never come to terms with how she felt about having a daughter with asthma. Jackie's logical self knew that she was not responsible for Poppy's illness, and that there was a good chance that Poppy would grow out of her asthma as she got older. But somehow Jackie's emotional self felt she should be able to help her daughter more – as if *she* were to blame for the asthma. Some of this guilt had been played out on Roger.

When Jackie returned home, she told Roger of some of the feelings she had. Roger said he felt he had coped with Poppy's asthma by trying *not* to feel emotional, and he explained that this may have made him seem cool towards Jackie. They both felt that trying to talk things through had helped them considerably. They were able to 'own up' to the emotions of the situation, rather than trying to repress them and then have them re-emerge as negative feelings towards each other.

Jackie and Roger passed through some elements of the change cycle. At first they were unaware of the change that Poppy's illness had made on their relationship. Jackie gradually realized that things were different since Poppy's diagnosis, but was unable to explain exactly what she felt, except to feel frustrated with Roger (stages 1 and 2). Talking to her mother helped Jackie to make sense of her feelings, and to decide to take action (stage 3). After talking to Roger, they were both able to see how they had avoided thinking about how Poppy's asthma had affected them as a couple. This led to an increased sense of closeness between them, and some practical changes. Roger agreed to comfort Poppy more at those times when he was at home. He discovered that this created a special bond between himself and Poppy, and he went on to join the local Asthma Support Group (stage 4).

Jackie and Roger could not control Poppy's illness. Obviously, they could take personal decisions about not smoking in her presence, or avoiding polluted atmospheres, but mostly her asthma was unexpected and beyond their personal control. However, what they could do was to understand the effect of her illness on them as individuals, and on them as a couple. This enabled them to give Poppy the real help she needed, rather than get caught in a muddle of feelings that might have eventually meant that the necessary focus on Poppy's health was lost.

Illness in the family

1 Illness can bring up all sorts of complex feelings, and to some extent these depend on the severity of the illness. Sometimes coping with a bad attack of flu can be enough to cause a couple to change the way in which they relate, and enough to promote tension over even a brief period of time. For instance, if you have a relationship where one partner is perceived as 'stronger' (either physically or emotionally) than the other, then if the stronger one is ill, it can feel threatening to the 'basics' (Chapter 1) on which the relationship is built. It may feel hard to swap roles, and both partners may feel resentful of each other. Sometimes this can be quite a positive exchange for a couple in that they may have an opportunity to explore another side of themselves, and therefore feel able to fulfil another role for their partner. However, you are likely to run through the change cycle before realizing the full value of these changes.

2 The natural emotions of anger and sadness at the illness, especially if it is more serious, may be quashed by both of you. It can be easy to feel sympathetic towards a partner for a short period of time, but if you have to deal with job loss because of the illness, or worry about your partner's health over a long period, the stress may be hard to handle. It is not unusual to feel a low-grade tension that manifests itself in biting remarks, or a loss of connectedness with your partner.

Case history
Sarah felt this when her boyfriend, Liam, developed a worrying ligament problem in his leg. He had always been a keen cricketer, but found he had to have operations on his leg and to give up his hopes of playing cricket at a professional level. They also had to put off moving into a house they had bought together because Liam couldn't manage to climb the stairs. Liam's problems also meant that they rarely went out together, and had to be very careful about where they went in case Liam couldn't sit or stand comfortably.

Sarah began by being understanding, but as the months went by she began to feel unhappy. She was worried about Liam, but also angry that their plans for the future had been spoilt. Sarah felt she couldn't say this to Liam – it seemed so self-centred when he was coping with so much discomfort. But she sometimes rowed with Liam, and these rows often centred around the leg exercises that his physiotherapist had set for him. Sarah felt he wasn't doing as many exercises as the hospital wanted him to. Liam would become angry and annoyed with Sarah at what he saw as her nagging, and they were soon caught in a circular argument, which often ended with no resolution and long silences.

Eventually Sarah spoke to the physiotherapist, who picked up on Sarah's anger. She asked Sarah about her feelings, and Sarah admitted she felt angry. It was the first time she had been able to admit her own feelings of disappointment at Liam's injury. The physiotherapist urged her to tell Liam, and – with some trepidation – she did so. Liam was also angry because he felt Sarah was saying she was angry with him for something he had no control over. He voiced his own deep sense of frustration over his loss of cricketing by telling Sarah it was really hard for him. Things between them were difficult for some time, and they split up for a while. But Sarah came to visit him when he had more surgery, and they talked about the loss they had both had to come to terms with. This enabled them to start again.

3 You may feel frozen in your development as a couple. As with Sarah and Liam, you may feel unable to move forward into a deeper relationship, or go backwards into something less committed, or even to split up. I have sometimes met couples who have stayed together during periods of crisis because it seemed thoughtless to part when one partner (or someone in the partner's family) falls ill. Some even get married instead of facing the truth about the viability of the partnership. This can lead to feelings of entrapment further on down the line. Of course, some relationships are strengthened by pulling together through illness, but it is important to realize the dangers of soldiering on when it might be braver to acknowledge the reality of the situation.

4 You may feel torn in your loyalties towards your partner. This is especially true if the sick person is a close relative, and you have to give up lots of time to care for them rather than spending time with your partner. These feelings can be most prevalent if the relative is an older person or a child, where you are both aware that care may be needed over an extended period of time.

Coping with Illness in the family

• Untangle what you can change, and what you cannot change. For instance, if your aged mother needs visiting regularly, does the visitor always need to be you? I am not suggesting that you abandon your mother, but daily visits can be exhausting and stressful if you have to travel long distances. Perhaps you could devise a system of visiting with other members of the family, which would both share the care and help you to feel supported. I have known couples who have told me that no one else can do the visiting or caring, but who, when asked, have never suggested other relatives might help because they thought they 'should have noticed without being told'. In many cases, the other relatives helped willingly once they realized the stress that the couple were under.

- Make use of all the support you need. Don't be afraid to talk to your GP, social worker or health visitor. Check out local support groups for illnesses, and carers, in your local area. Be honest with friends about your worries, and ask them to help you. They may be just the right person to offer a shoulder to cry on, or a night's babysitting so that you and your partner can see each other.
- Talk about the feelings you are going through. You and your partner may argue sometimes, but you may also manage to work out tension and sadness. You could start by explaining to your partner that you understand that much of the problem cannot be changed, but that you need to talk through the feelings you have so that you can cope with the future.
- Avoid being sacrificial. When someone is ill, it can be tempting to sacrifice yourself to meet their need.

Case history
Emmie and Ashley found themselves in this situation when Emmie developed ME – sometimes called Chronic fatigue Syndrome. Emmie gave up her job, while Ashley stayed at the factory he had always worked at. During lunch breaks he dashed home to cook for Emmie, and spent weekends frantically trying to keep up with all that needed doing at home. He missed his friends, and was soon dropped from the darts team he had been a member of. Gradually all the fun in his life fell away, and he found himself either working at the factory, or working at home. He became exhausted, both emotionally and physically. He also felt isolated, and had times when he wondered if he and Emmie would stay together. Emmie did improve, but they both faced a struggle to get their relationship, and their social life, back on course again.

Emmie and Ashley illustrate the need to nurture yourself as individuals, and as a couple, when illness strikes. Imagine yourself as two large pots. Your fun life, or relaxation time, fills one pot, and the other pot acts as a container for your worries and concerns. This pot has holes it, and empties quickly, often leaking over the rest of your life. You can use the pot full of relaxation and time to refresh the side of you that is worried or busy. For a short while, you could even dip into the pot to keep you going when times are tough. However, if you take from your relaxation pot for too long, without refilling, there will eventually be nothing left and you will grind to a halt. The leaky pot of stress will continue to drip on you, but you will have nothing to dilute the feelings, or to draw on if things get much worse. This is why being too self-sacrificing can eventually end up with both of you feeling ill, rather than one supporting the other.

This last point is a difficult one to accept, but may help you. Just as relationships have cycles of change, so do our bodies. These days it is common to believe that illness is an aberration of normal life. You may believe that everything has a cure, and that trying to accept illness as part of normal human life is defeatist and unhelpful. Yet many people do experience pain or disability every single day, and they are not any less human because of this. If you are faced with a long-term illness, you may both feel as if your life should be suspended until it goes away. In reality you may have to accept the illness as part of your relationship, just as you would any other change. You may have to work through the cycle of change, but this would still happen if the change was more positive – if you won the lottery, for instance! Fight the parts that can be fought, and allow yourself to accept the parts that cannot be changed. If you have to have a leg amputated, no amount of wishing will replace the leg. You can fight to learn to walk again, but you will still have to learn how to be one-legged.

Bereavement

Did you have bereavement lessons at school? I ask this because I feel that understanding death has taken over from sex as the greater taboo in society. If you had any help with understanding death at school, the chances are it was very limited, and didn't receive the same sort of attention that science or maths did. Yet this is the one thing we can be certain of in life – that we will encounter death somehow, and eventually die ourselves.

Perhaps the first time you met with death was when your pet died. Try to think how this was handled for you. I sometimes ask couples about this if they seem to be having difficulties with a bereavement. Their answers cover a huge range of experience. Some tell me that their pet budgie seemed to live for ever, only for them to discover once grown up that their parents had replaced it with an identical bird when it died. Others were callously told that their dog had died, and how good it would be not to have mess around the house. Some had pets that 'disappeared', or went to 'visit' some far-flung relative, when in fact they had been put to sleep. Others told me of touching ceremonies when even goldfish were given a ceremonial burial service. This may seem an odd start to thinking about bereavement, but how you responded to losing a pet, and what you learnt from the way the loss was handled, can help you to make sense of the way in which bereavement touches the life of a couple. Tragically, some people know only too well how bereavement can feel from experiencing the loss of a parent (or other close relative or friend) in childhood.

Bereavement can also follow a pattern of response (similar to the cycle of change). People tend to see this as a straight line, but it rarely works in this way. Most people find they move in and out of the various phases of feeling, and revisit certain thoughts and emotions over and over again. Here are some of the feelings that you may experience, either alone or as a couple:

1 A sense of numbness and shock

You may feel as if you are cut off from normal life, or carry on as if nothing has happened, wondering why those around you are behaving so strangely. (My grandmother dusted and cleaned the whole house on the day we suffered a bereavement in our home.) The sense of shock can also bring with it physical symptoms, such as shaking and trembling, or feeling especially cold or hot. Your partner may wonder if you have really understood the reality of the death, and feel unable to 'reach' you. You may also be aware of watching events as if you were a stranger, with no real involvement in them.

2 The need to weep

Not everybody feels the desire to weep, although it can be very cleansing to allow yourself to cry. Understanding and being with a partner who cries seems to depend on how tears are usually handled in the relationship. Some couples can share tears, while others see them as embarrassing. Some couples have told me that sharing tears has helped them to feel closer to their partner.

3 Anger

Anger is one of the most unacknowledged emotions during bereavement. Crying, feeling sad, being withdrawn or becoming depressed are all commonly seen as acceptable, while anger is often seen as inappropriate. However, anger is important in the grieving process, for it can help people to get rid of the overwhelming feeling of being rejected by the dead person. This sounds illogical, and in a way it is, but when a loved one dies it can feel as if they have left you deliberately. It is not unusual to experience anger at any point after a death. Doctors and nurses often report relatives angrily demanding to know what more could have been done to help a terminally ill patient, while vicars often have to deal with grieving relatives railing at God, or simply asking why their relative had to die. As the partner of someone grieving, you may end up on the receiving end of anger that has nowhere else to go. This can cause your relationship to feel strained just at the point when you need to feel supported.

4 Periods of depression, and a sense of being cut out of your partner's life

If you are the one who is grieving, you may feel unable to articulate your feelings, or just feel there is no point in talking at all. This is normal if it comes and goes, but if the feelings last a long time, in yourself or your partner, then it may be time to seek help. Your GP or Cruse (the bereavement counselling agency) could help you through this time.

5 Longing for life to be as it was before the death

You may wish you could have said goodbye, told the person who has died how much you loved them, or even have said 'sorry' for any unresolved issues between you. This period of yearning can be particularly acute at anniversaries connected to the dead person, such as birthdays, Christmas, the anniversary of their death or family gatherings. Sometimes this yearning can cause you to believe the dead person has 'returned'. Many bereaved people report 'seeing' or 'hearing' the dead person in the months following the death. Some people see this as comforting, while others feel afraid. Others see it as evidence of an afterlife. Whatever you believe, it is experienced by lots of bereaved people, and it usually passes after some months.

Coping with death – for you and your partner

Numbness and shock

This an almost universal experience for most people after experiencing bereavement and can best be coped with by waiting for the reality of the death to be experienced. If you force yourself, or your partner, to 'face up to' what has happened, you run the risk of never truly letting go of the dead person. You both need time to assimilate what has happened, and the shock period is a natural way in which the body responds to stressful circumstances. You can help by offering practical support, such as allowing your partner to rest, and dealing with the myriad of immediate concerns – such as fielding phone calls and visitors, contacting funeral directors, or dealing with the hospital if the person died after an illness.

Sadness and Tears

It can be tempting to try to stem tears by distracting the person who is crying. This can take various forms, from rushing off to make a cup of tea, to telling them to 'pull themselves together'. This kind of reaction usually only serves to block the natural process of grieving, and can make things much worse for the bereaved person. It is better to sit with them and allow the tears to flow. It can help to offer a hug, but be led by their need to be comforted rather than your need to comfort. There is no need to say much. In fact, a supportive silence can be just as helpful as particular words.

If you do talk, try reflecting what you see and hear. For instance, if your partner is struggling to speak through sobs, you can say something like 'it seems very hard for you to talk to me because you feel so sad'. This probably sounds banal in written form, but has the important effect of helping the unhappy person to feel you understand what they are going through. You or your partner will have good days and bad days, and you may find yourself in tears many months or years after a bereavement. (These kind of feelings of sadness can often be triggered by something small – perhaps a favourite shared song, or by doing something you always did with the person who has died.) It is unhelpful to chastise your partner, or yourself, by saying 'you should be over that by now'. After all, if you cared at all for the dead person, then they deserve your grief. This can also be true even if you didn't get on well with the person who has died. In these circumstances, your tears may represent a grieving for the relationship you never had, and can help you to come to terms with the loss of both the real person, and the person you wanted.

Anger

If you can accept that angry feelings are natural after a death, then you will be a long way towards coping with the anger. If your grieving partner picks arguments with you, or keeps saying the doctor was negligent, when you know there really was no hope, then you will cope better if you don't respond angrily yourself. Use the reflection process that I described when dealing with sadness. Say something like, 'You seem angry and upset that the doctor didn't do as much as you hoped could be done'. It is probably not helpful to argue the case with someone who is feeling this way, as the anger is not really directed at you (or the doctor), but at the injustice of the death itself. It is better to tackle the anger when your partner is not actually showing their anger. Pick a time when you can talk, and explain how you feel about the anger that comes your way. Use 'I feel . . .' at the beginning of your statements, as in Chapter 4. You could try something like 'I feel hurt/sad/confused [or whatever seems appropriate] when you shout at me over things I feel have little to do with me. I feel as if you are angry with [the dead person, or God, or life in general], but showing that anger to me'. At first, you may be met with resistance to this idea, but if you keep trying to help your partner to understand where the anger comes from, they will gradually cope better with the angry emotions. In some ways, this is similar to the 'cycle of change' I explained in Chapter 1. You will have to work through these changes in relationship to the death in the same way as other changes.

Depression and low moods

In thinking about depression after death, it is important to understand the difference between depression that needs more help than the support of a loving partner, and simply feeling low and unhappy. You should seek help for your partner (or yourself) if you notice that your partner is:

- Having trouble sleeping, and often wakes early in the morning and seems unable to get back to sleep.
- Is tired and lethargic.
- Takes less interest in themselves. For instance, they may not wash or dress properly, or eat regularly.
- Talks about suicide, or seems to have a plan of intent to kill themselves.
- Stops communicating with you, and seems distant and unresponsive to events around them.
- Seems to have been this way for a long period of time – possibly weeks or months.

These indications may suggest that your partner (or you yourself) may be suffering from a clinical depression, that needs medical treatment. Consult your GP, and explain all the problems you or your partner have encountered.

The problem with depression following a death is that it may look like a deep-seated depression that needs help, when it is really the bereaved person coming to terms with their loss. Perhaps the best indicator is the length of time it goes on. It is likely that a grieving person wil experience some, or all, of the above symptoms of depression as they cope with their loss, but they will probably go through some of the other stages we have mentioned.

You can help someone who is in a low mood by encouraging them to talk about the death. Bereaved people often feel the need to tell the 'story' of the death over and over again. It can be helpful for them to tell you from the beginning how they first heard about the death, what they did next, and how the funeral went and who came to see them. You can also help them by encouraging them to talk about the dead person. You could use simple aids such as photographs or letters to remind them of the importance of the person who has died. Be sensitive to their needs; don't force this approach, but allow the dead person to be a natural part of their life, rather than hidden away as a taboo subject.

Longing and yearning

You can help in this area by allowing your partner (or yourself) to acknowledge and understand why they long for the dead person to return. The ache inside can be almost physical, and can feel overwhelming at times. Sometimes a grieving person can be helped by writing down their thoughts and emotions. Head a piece of paper 'If [name of dead person] were still alive, this is what I would want to say to them', or 'I would say this if [my mother/friend/uncle etc.] were still alive'. This can especially help if the relationship was not always easy or straightforward, and there are elements of guilt left behind.

Guilt is a common reaction after a death, and can occur over even seemingly unimportant things. I once saw a woman in counselling who was wracked with guilt because she had not changed her husband's bed sheets the night before he died. This kind of guilt can be linked to longing for the return of the dead person by the person close to them, and a fear that somehow the death was the result of a lack of attention or love on their behalf. This can be especially true for children affected by death who may believe that their relative has 'gone away' because they were bad or naughty. It can be helped by asking the bereaved person to talk through why they feel guilty. In the case of the woman who was guilty over the bed sheets, I asked her to tell me why this had affected her so badly. She told me it was because she wanted him to die in comfort, and that she had worried all along that he had been in more pain than he admitted to. She knew she could do little about the pain, but the sheets were in her control, so she kept them clean to show him how much she loved him. I asked her if she had been able to tell him she loved him. She said she had told him just before he died, and she realized she had shared her love in more important ways than changing the sheets. She was then able to let go of the feelings she had carried about the guilt, and grieve for the loss of her husband in a less confused way.

Your relationship may be knocked by death or illness, but these things can be seen as part of the cycle of change. Instead of viewing them as events that must be feared, or shut away in the mind as 'something we will never have to cope with', you can use this chapter to help you prepare for those things you may have little control over, or to help you deal with them once they have happened. In the next chapter, we will be looking at how relationships break down, and what to do if you think this may be going to happen to you – or has already happened to you.

9

Breakdown in Your Relationship

The previous chapters in this book have mainly been concerned with maintaining a close relationship through the cycle of change. However, there are times when a relationship has to end, and acknowledging this can be very difficult. You may feel that if you could try harder, or wait longer, the relationship could be improved. It is a difficult thing to appreciate when you are stuck in the middle of a painful parting, but ending a relationship and moving on to another life is still part of the change circle – rather like a wheel within a wheel. This understanding takes a long time to achieve, and you may wonder if you will ever get over the sadness and anger that this kind of breakdown causes.

As a counsellor, I know that many couples come to see me at the last possible moment. They are usually at a crisis point – perhaps about to split up, or already living apart. Sometimes they will have been struggling with one of the crunch points I have already written about, such as parenting problems, money worries, sexual concerns or affairs. They often tell me they did not see the crisis coming; or that even if they had, they wouldn't have known how to take action to prevent the crack between them widening into a chasm.

Many of the difficulties that can cause a couple to part are the same ones that many other couples tussle with. However, some couples cope with these, while others seem to fall apart very quickly. So how can you spot the indicators that your relationship is in serious trouble, and what action could you take to stop yourself and your partner drifting further apart?

Spotting serious problems

Communication changes

Perhaps you and your partner are now keeping more and more feelings to yourselves. You may also develop secret feelings towards your partner; these could range from uncertainty about how you feel towards them, to total distrust. You are likely to be aware that issues you would have willingly discussed in the past are now 'taboo'; you may believe you could predict your partner's unfavourable response to a difficult subject. You could begin to find it easier to confide in someone else – a close friend or relative.

Lack of shared 'basics'

You may feel that you no longer share the same 'basics'. This is more common in couples who are initially drawn together by a strong shared sense of being a 'special couple'. Couples like this can feel bound together because they believe that the world doesn't understand them in the way they understand each other. For instance, they may be very young in making a committed relationship, and face the opposition of parents, or feel intensely connected by work or study. This immediate connection may fade with time (the young couple grow older, and the couple linked by work change jobs), and the powerful sense of connection can feel threatened. This can lead to feelings of disillusionment, and echoes stage 4 in Chapter 2 when couples begin to understand about the whole of their partner.

Blaming and defending

You may find it hard to listen to your partner without being extremely defensive, or when you talk to your partner they seem to erect an invisible barrier that you cannot get through, no matter what you do. Perhaps you notice that you or your partner blame each other a great deal. In other words, you disown personal responsibility for difficulties, and see it all as your partner's fault. This usually leads to arguments that go round and round in circles, and never reach a satisfactory conclusion.

Fear of openness

You may have recently been through a crisis, such as an affair, and found this difficult to talk about. You may both be conscious of pushing some unresolved issues 'under the carpet'. If any of this contentious material were to be exposed, you fear a great chasm could open up between you.

Detachment

As a couple, you may sense some detachment. What fascinated you in the past now seems uninteresting. If your partner tells you about something they have been involved in, you may experience a feeling of 'couldn't care less'. Some couples that I've seen describe this sensation as seeing their partner through a stranger's eyes. It is as if the web of connections, both personal and public, has fallen away, and you no longer feel close to one another.

Sexual problems

Sex seems to be less satisfactory, and has been this way for several months. You may suffer from a loss of libido, or feel unattracted to your partner. You could develop sexual problems as described in Chapter 5. However, sexual difficulties are not always linked to relationship problems, so you should visit your GP if you are concerned about this.

Case history
Natasha and Saba experienced these feelings over the period when they were splitting up. Natasha was a rep. for a tour operator, and had met Saba while working in North Africa. Despite their difficult cultural backgrounds, they had fallen in love and eventually married. They decided to try to live in England, and finally settled down after a period when they were anxious about whether Saba would be able to stay. At first, they felt very close to one another. Natasha felt protective towards Saba as she helped him learn about the customs in her country, and Saba was grateful for her help.

However, as Natasha continued to travel, Saba felt more and more dissatisfied with being alone. Natasha began to avoid sex with Saba, and Saba found it more and more difficult to talk to her about anything deeper than everyday life. What had seemed effortless in the early days of their relationship now seemed uncomfortable and infrequent. Natasha talked to her sister about Saba, and the way she felt, and realized she could no longer share things with Saba in the way she could with her sister. Natasha and Saba began to argue constantly, and Natasha eventually left him. She felt disillusioned and sad that what had seemed a good marriage had faltered so quickly.

Natasha and Saba experienced the feelings of loss and detachment that many couples describe when splitting up. Of course, it is also possible to experience all these feelings during the lifetime of a committed relationship.

Some of the list above could be described as symptoms of the change cycle. However, if you find yourself stuck in any of them for a long period of time, or realize that gradually all these feelings are true for you, then you need to take action. It may be that you can both commit yourself to changing the decay in the partnership, or it could mean deciding whether the relationship has a future at all.

Reclaiming the relationship

Although it may seem a painful proposition, you need to try to talk about the issues that have been pushed aside. You can do this by:

- Avoiding blaming. If you start every conversation with an accusation, your partner will switch off and nothing will be resolved.
- Stop trying to prove your point of view during rows; most rows solve very little. Often the real resolution begins after the row, when some of the fire has been spent.
- Be honest about your very real concerns about the relationship. Tell your partner that you wonder if the relationship can survive if it goes on the way it is. Don't say something like, 'I'm off if you don't mend your ways'. Instead, talk about the relationship, and your feelings.
- Be specific about what the problem is. Say, 'We used to be able to tell each other anything, but now I'm finding it difficult to tell you what I did today', rather than, 'You never talk to me any more'.
- Listen to your partner carefully, and give them time to express their opinion. You may disagree, but you need to hear all they have to say in order to be open in return.
- Go back to your 'basics', and see if any of them remain in the relationship. If they have declined, or remained so fixed you cannot believe in them any more, then think about whether they can be remade.
- Put time aside to spend together. Get to know each other as you are today, rather than how you were when you fell in love.

If you begin to feel your relationship is in trouble, make an appointment to see a counsellor who specializes in couple issues. Relate has centres across the country with trained relationship counsellors who could help you to decide what future there may be for your relationship. All Relate counsellors abide by a code of confidentiality and the British Association of Counselling code of ethnics. They are supervised by qualified Relate supervisors. Payment is negotiable, and no one is ever turned away on the grounds of inability to pay. However, if you decide to go for any form of counselling, there are some important questions to ask your counsellor before trusting them with your worries. You should check out the following things:

1 What form of counselling they are qualified in, and how long ago they qualified. Ask to see any relevant certification. If they are in training, they should tell you.
2 Whether they are undergoing regular supervision with a qualified supervisor. All counsellors should attend supervision for themselves – either in a group, or as individuals. This is to ensure 'quality control' of counselling, and to prevent your abuse by a counsellor who is not practising as they should be.

3 Ask if they abide by the British Association for Counselling code of ethnics, or some other code of ethics (such as the British Association for Sexual and Marital Therapy). Ask for a copy of the code of ethics, so that you can read what your rights are while in counselling.
4 Check whether they have a reliable complaints procedure, and personal insurance in the event of you making a complaint. In some senses, this is the responsibility of the counsellor, but you could feel more secure if you know the full situation.
5 Enquire how much the fees are, and if there is any negotiation available within the fee scale.
6 Ask for a review session to be scheduled after a certain number of sessions. It is very difficult to judge how long counselling will be, but it is wise to have a review session to help you budget ahead, rather than be sucked into a long series of sessions, during which the cost can mount considerably.

NEVER seek help from a counsellor who wants you to do anything you feel is abusive. If he or she suggests any form of sexual touching, or tries to coerce you into doing something they think is a good idea, but *you* are worried about, then stop the counselling. Seek help from the association that they claim to follow if you think this has happened to you.

Common responses to the end of a relationship

Case history
Kim and Josh had been married for seven years when they split up. They had one child, a 2-year-old daughter called Lin. Kim had been married before, and had met and married Josh very quickly after her divorce. They had been attracted to each other instantly, and had enjoyed an intense sexual relationship at the beginning of the relationship. Neither foresaw the arguments that began after they had been married for about 16 months. Mostly the rows were about trivial issues such as who did the housework and the shopping. They also argued about sex, which seemed to have lost its spark. Josh especially felt that every time they were together, they rowed. He wanted to have a happier, less bitter relationship with Kim, but no matter how much he tried, they just returned to fighting.

When they realized Kim was pregnant, they were very shocked. Both had privately been contemplating leaving the relationship, but now felt trapped by the baby. They made a renewed effort to recreate the closeness they had once had, but neither really believed in their partnership any longer. The arguments had made them feel wary of commitment to each other, and they parted some time later. Both felt bitter, hurt and disillusioned. Kim particularly felt angry that she had been through another broken marriage. At first she blamed Josh, but then felt depressed and miserable. She and Josh still saw each other because Josh visited Lin, their daughter, most weeks. Kim felt a confusing mixture of rage and longing when Josh visited. Josh experienced very similar emotions, and had to force himself to go on taking Lin out. Every time he called at Kim's new flat, he found himself wanting to see Kim, but also wanting to run away. They often snapped at each other during these brief encounters.

As the months went by, Josh realized he had almost cut himself off from his friends. He had felt so consumed by the divorce, and coping with its aftermath, that he had simply worked and slept. Now he began to accept invitations from friends to go out again. He felt strange going out without Kim, and described this to a friend as 'like being 16 again'. He felt awkward, and had to 'relearn' how to relate to a woman. At times, he still found himself wanting to be with Kim – even though things had been so difficult at the end of the marriage. He still remembered the early days of their relationship, and regretted the way it had died. Gradually he rebuilt a life without Kim, and the desire to go back faded. He was able to see that there had been good times with Kim, but they had not outweighed the rows and unhappiness that had grown between them.

Kim took longer to come through the split. The break-up had caused her to doubt herself, and whether she would manage alone again. She spent a lot of time with her mother, who had helped her through her first divorce. She cried a lot, often at night, and had difficulty in sleeping. Kim felt puzzled by this reaction. She told herself she had chosen to divorce, and that she shouldn't be feeling so low. She also had to contend with caring for Lin, who often asked to see her father. Kim felt she couldn't explain this properly to Lin. One day, Lin asked Kim if Daddy 'didn't live with them because she had been a naughty girl'. Kim was often tired, and worried about Lin. She had returned to work as a librarian and, although she enjoyed this, wondered if she was working as well as she ought. She sometimes made mistakes, and was afraid she might lose her job.

Kim was slower at returning to a social life than Josh. On one occasion she went out with a friend to a club and was asked to dance. She felt herself freeze with anxiety, and then left early. She was bruised by her two broken marriages and, although she had not fully realized this, knew she needed plenty of time to recover. She also wondered if she and Josh could revive the early, intense bond they had shared. In her heart, though, she knew this was not possible. Kim recognized a repeat of some of the feelings she had been through at the end of her previous marriage. Perhaps the biggest difference was that at the end of her first marriage she had thrown herself into a lot of new relationships, of which Josh had been the last.

Both Josh and Kim found the actual act of ending their marriage much more difficult than they had ever thought it would be. Well over a year later, they still felt depressed at times, and Josh especially went through a difficult emotional period later than Kim. He found himself feeling lonely, and regretting the divorce. Josh felt his work suffered at this point and, having taken some steps back into socializing, he retreated into spending evenings alone. Eventually, three years on, Josh and Kim felt they had survived their split. It had been much more painful than they could have predicted, and both felt it had left mental scars.

Josh and Kim illustrate the effects of divorce over a long period of time. It is not uncommon for me to counsel people who say, 'It's been a year since my divorce. Why do I feel so bad, and shouldn't I be over it by now?' My answer to this is to say that divorce has a similar emotional impact to bereavement. In fact, some people feel it is worse. If a partner dies, there is a straightforward end, and the person who dies has not usually chosen to die. Divorce can feel desperately painful because one or both people in the marriage have chosen the ending. A responsible relationship may have to be maintained because of children who will continue to need parenting by both parents. The pain of seeing an ex-partner can be very hard to bear, particularly if they have found a new partner.

Common after-effects of divorce

Shock

Although you may have realized that the end was inevitable, you can still feel shocked that you are facing a divorce; if your partner has asked for a divorce when you thought the marriage was happy, the sense of shock will be much more intense. Alongside the shock, you may experience disbelief that the marriage has ended.

Anger and blaming

You may both want to blame each other, and feel a desire to distance yourself from any personal feelings that suggest you had a part in the breakdown. You are also likely to feel angry, and rows at this time can be particularly bitter. An alternative of blame towards the other partner can be self-blame, which may involve you repeatedly asking yourself whether you did something to cause the breakdown, or to cause your partner to want a divorce.

Euphoria

If the relationship has been particularly acrimonious, you may feel 'set free'. This can induce a feeling of being almost 'high', and you could behave differently – perhaps buying new clothes and losing weight in an effort to create a 'new you'. This feeling of euphoria can be followed by a dip down into sadness as you take in the reality of the situation.

Sadness and loss

Like coping with a death, you may find yourself crying and unable to carry out your normal daily routine. You could lose weight, or comfort-eat. You may also feel lost without your normal pattern of being in a couple, and yearn for what has been lost, even if the relationship was unhappy.

Confusion

You may wonder what the future holds, and how you are both going to manage the complexity of uncoupling – from managing the split of your home and property, to ensuring that the children will continue to see both of you. You may find that this leads you to feeling unable to think about the simplest issues, or makes it hard to absorb instructions about splitting property.

A desire for revenge

This is a common feeling among those who have been left by a partner who has a new relationship, or who admits a past affair. Some people do act on this desire (there have been some famous revenge cases in the past). This is understandable; nobody wants to be deceived and then abandoned. However, retribution can have a backlash on the revenger. You may later feel embarrassed by your actions, or cause hostility between you and your ex-partner just when you need to retain communication for the sake of any children you may have. Children who watch and absorb parental conflict are more likely to be traumatized by divorce than those whose parents handle parting with the minimum of anger.

A return of teenage emotions

Like Josh and Kim, you may feel like a teenager again, with the same awkwardness and excitement about meeting new people you may have last felt in your adolescence. Some people rush into new relationships, and experiment sexually. This can sometimes be caused by a desire to 'prove' themselves attractive after the rejection of divorce.

Delayed reaction

Some couples get through the break-up relatively smoothly, but then suffer many of the above feelings some months (or even years) later. For some couples, the practical matters connected with breaking up demand so much attention that their emotional response gets put 'on hold'. Later, these feelings catch up with them, and they may come for counselling feeling puzzled at their delayed sadness or anger.

Inability to concentrate on work

One of the commonest responses to any kind of traumatic change is the inability to concentrate. Some research on the effect of divorce on men and women suggests that men seem to do less well in keeping work and everyday life going. Women are more likely to pick up the threads of their working life more quickly, but this may be because of employers' response to women, which can be more sympathetic than the response that men receive. Men are often thought to be able to 'pull themselves together' quickly, and those who show signs of problems can find themselves helped less rather than more.

Other effects can be a loss of friendships, esecially those people who knew you as a couple. These friends may find it hard to know what to say, or how to relate to you as a single person. You can smooth the way by explaining how you are feeling, and ask them for their support. If you move to a new house or community, you may feel lost and uncertain about your decision. Try to seek help from supportive groups in the area – from parent and child groups, school-based groups or the local community centre. If you have any financial or legal concerns, contact the local Citizens' Advice Bureau; they will either help you personally, or refer you to an expert locally. They are especially helpful with benefit enquiries.

All of the responses I have described are normal and if you go through a separation, there will also be many responses that will be unique to you. However, if you or your partner feels very depressed or withdrawn, or even suicidal, then you should seek help as soon as possible. You GP is your best first point of contact. He or she will be able to offer you medication or other help (such as counselling) to alleviate your feelings.

Children and divorce or separation

Children need special help in dealing with their parents' divorce or separation. I often see couples who believe that the best policy is to keep their children in ignorance about the step they are about to take. In some ways, this is understandable: parents protect children by shielding them from difficult issues until they are old enough to understand the implications. That is why we have age limits on films at the cinema, and laws to protect the young from exploitation.

Unfortunately, children of divorcing parents are not helped by parents who say nothing until the decree absolute. Children are equipped with antennae that begin operating at birth. They can often sense changes in mood and emotion in parents without ever being told directly. If a mother or father says nothing, but the child senses coldness or anger in their parents' relationship, they may blame themselves for causing the separation. Children (as Lin did in Josh's and Kim's case) often assume that it is because they have been naughty, not done well enough at school, or broke a window last month. Yet in telling children nothing, we are not protecting them. In fact, you may simply be doing this to protect yourself from facing the truth – that the relationship is over. One of the saddest stories I heard from an adult survivor of divorce was her memories of childhood. She told me how she spent most nights in bed, hiding under her blanket, listening to her parents fighting downstairs. There was no physical violence, but they screamed and shouted constantly. Even as an adult, she could not escape the feeling that she had somehow been responsible for their rows. Her father often yelled at her mother that he would 'leave if it wasn't for her children'. The rows were never spoken of, and it had prevented my client from making a successful relationship herself. She feared that all relationships eventually ended up full of anger and recrimination.

How children deal with relationship breakdown

Children respond to their parents' relationship breakdown in different ways. Some children take things in their stride and appear unaffected. Others respond by being extremely unhappy, angry or uncommunicative. You will know what is natural for your child, and what seems unusual behaviour. However, there are some common themes of behaviour in children, which are often age-related.

Babies to age 3

Children of these ages may become 'clingy', perhaps hanging on to their mother when they have been beginning to venture out on their own. You may notice your children behaving differently over everyday routines. For example, they may take longer to eat their breakfast, or refuse to go to bed. They may cry more easily than usual, or be more silent than is normal for them. If your estranged partner comes to visit them, or take them out, they may push them away, or seem bewildered at the changes.

Ages 3 to 5

Children of this age often behave as if they are younger than they really are. They could return to bed-wetting or thumb sucking. They can also be reluctant to go anywhere without the parent they have been left with, and may hang on tightly to their parent if being left at playschool. Children who have previously settled well at a childminder, or nursery, may return to crying and asking for their parent.

It is common for children of this age to blame themselves. Sometimes they will try to put this into words (as with Natasha's and Josh's little girl, Lin), or they can feel or think they are somehow to blame for Mum and Dad separating. Sometimes they may wonder if *they* could be 'sent away', especially if they have overheard one parent telling the other to go.

Ages 5 to 8

Children of this age often long for parents to return, and can delude themselves into believing that the missing parent will come back. They may try to manipulate parents into returning by asking parents to get back together, or promising to 'be good' if Mum or Dad will move back in. Children can suffer all the effects of grief and loss described under adults' responses earlier in the chapter.

Ages 9 to 11

Children of this age often see their parents as either devils or angels. They tend to blame one parent, and idealize the other. Often, the parent who has left is seen as the 'devil' and the carer parent as the 'angel'. However, this is not always so. Sometimes the parent who has left is seen as all good, and the parent they live with is blamed for driving the other away. Children in this age group may also appear to be older than their years, often comforting their parent. Boys tend to feel they have to replace their father if the father was the one to leave, and vice versa with girls.

Adolescence

The usual difficulties with adolescence may be exaggerated by parents who split up. Teenagers may find it hard to respect their parents, and behave as if they were older. Girls sometimes enter into inappropriate sexual relationships, or leave home quickly. Boys are more likely to challenge parental authority, and may have problems with discipline. Your child's school can help in this situation by keeping you in touch with any behaviour changes or problems. If the father has been the one to leave (most divorces still do involve the father going), adolescents may begin to ask about their father, and could even want to be with him more, or search for him if contact has been lost.

Adult offspring

It is common to imagine that once past the teens, the effect of parental separation is hardly felt. In fact, adult offspring can go through all the unhappiness that younger children experience. They may feel polarized into seeing one parent as good and one as bad. If the parents remarry, these emotions may only surface at the wedding, or when their parents meet a new partner. Adult offspring may feel unable to make relationships, and themselves fear break-up of partnerships. They can also feel angry and rejected, even though they are grown up and living away from their parents.

Helping children cope with relationship breakdown and separation

Keep children informed

Children need to know what is going on when a relationship ends, and there are some important dos and don'ts when talking to children about this painful time:

- Do adapt your language and explanation to the age of the child. Try to tell them in a way that they can understand easily; keep it simple.
- Don't give complicated reasons for the break-up. Just say what is going to happen in the near future, and how they are likely to be affected. The end of the relationship will be the first thing on *your* mind, but they may be worrying about whether they will be able to go to the same school.
- Don't blame your partner for leaving. Saying something like 'Daddy's gone because he can't love me any more' may be true as

far as you are concerned, but may cause the child to worry that
Daddy will stop loving her.
- Don't single out one child to tell alone. Where at all possible, tell
  them together, and with both you and your partner present.
- Do try to decide how you are going to tell the children. Practise
  answers to questions they are likely to ask.
- Do reassure and comfort them. Tell them that although you may not
  be living together, you are still their parents, and will care for them
  as parents throughout their lives.

Keep your promises

Children need continuity of care, and need to know that although your
relationship has changed, the love for them is still ongoing. If you
promise to see them, or take them to see an absent parent, then you
must do it. Children who are let down by broken promises can grow up
believing there is no one you can really trust. Younger children need
regular visits that are not too long. Sometimes, a whole day can be too
long, whereas an hour or two shared with the child more frequently can
help to maintain a feeling of trust. Older children can cope with longer
periods of contact. Don't try to fill their visits with special events; let
them do their usual activities if possible. Watching television together,
playing a computer game, or reading favourite stories can all help to
reassure the child that you are the same Mum or Dad you have always
been.

Be honest

I have sometimes met couples who decided to tell lies to their children
about their imminent split.

Case History
One couple told their two sons that Daddy was going away on a
business trip (a common occurrence for this family). When Daddy
didn't return for several weeks, both sons began to show signs of
great anxiety. One son even drew pictures of car crashes, and
eventually admitted to his mother that he thought his father had died
in a crash. The couple had believed that a 'clean break' was better all
round, but the boys needed to see their father, and to talk about the
confusion of feelings within. When he did return to visit them, the
boys were extremely angry with him, and it took months for them to
return to a reasonable relationship. Tell your children the truth;
shielding or deceiving them will have negative pay-offs in the
future.

Reassure them

Your children will need more understanding and affection from you. This doesn't mean buying gifts or special treats, but more patience. This will probably seem a tall order at a stage when you feel emotionally exhausted, but if they are to survive this time they need both of you to make the extra effort. Make sure they understand that the responsibility for the relationship ending is yours alone, not theirs.

Find your own support

Sometimes parents lean on their children for emotional support. This is a natural feeling, and happens after a death as well. It may be OK for a short time, but if children are forced into the 'carer' role because you have nobody to talk to, they may resent it in later life. It can also cause this kind of child 'carer' to end up 'caring' all their life, forming relationships with others who need 'putting back together'. Some partners of alcoholics and gamblers are like this – unable to lay down their caring role. Ask friends and relatives to support you, or seek counselling to help you deal with your feelings.

Ending a relationship is very hard. You will need great resilience to come through, but even separation and the changes it involves can have gains as well as losses. At the beginning of starting out alone, you will be like a miner in a diamond mine, scraping away in the dark. You will frequently scrape your knuckles, and diamonds will be few and far between. Gradually, you will see light, though, and the rewards will improve. You may never have chosen to be a 'miner', but you may discover more about yourself than you knew existed *if* you can reframe and embrace the differences you have faced.

Postscript

If you have read this book right through, you will know that there are ways to help you cope with crunch points and the change that they bring. Now that you have used the questions to understand how you have approached problems in the past, you can use this book to reshape how you will deal with worries in the future. My sincere hope is that your relationship will be stronger, and more able to deal with the cycle of change.

Helping Agencies

British Association for Counselling,
1 Regent Place,
Rugby,
CV21 2PJ.
Tel: 01788 550899

This agency can supply lists of counsellors in your local area. Contact them on the telephone number above to request a list. They will ask for a SAE.

British Association for Sexual and Marital Therapy,
PO Box 62,
Sheffield,
S10 3TS.

This organization mainly deals with the accreditation of counsellors and therapists, and works towards educating the public on matters of sexual and marital therapy.

Cruse (Bereavement Care),
Cruse House,
126 Sheen Road,
Richmond,
Surrey,
TW9 1UR.
Tel: 0181 940 4818
Bereavement line: 0181 332 7227

Cruse offers help to all bereaved people via its 192 branches. Group and individual counselling is available across the country.

Cry-sis Support Group,
BM CRY-SIS,
London,
WC1N 3XX.
Tel: 0171 404 5011 (daily 8 a.m.–11 p.m.)

Cry-sis aims to provide emotional and practical support to parents of babies who cry a great deal. They also have a national network of self-help groups.

Exploring Parenthood,
4 Ivory Place,
20a Treadgold St.,
London,
W11 4BP.
Tel: 0171 221 4471
Parents' advice line: 0171 221 6681

This group offers an advice line, open to all parents (whether adoptive or those with disabled children). It also offers group counselling and discussions on parenting.

Family Planning Association,
Margaret Pyke House,
27–35 Mortimer Street,
London,
W1N 7RJ.
Tel: 0171 636 7866

The Family Planning Association offers educative leaflets to the public on a wealth of sexual health issues, and a national service on contraception. Local clinics are listed in the phone book.

Gingerbread,
16–17 Clerkenwell Close,
London,
EC1R 0AA.
Tel: 0171 336 8183
0171 336 8184 (Advice Line)

Gingerbread offers day-to-day support for lone parents. They have 250 local groups that meet regularly, and offer an advice line (number above) through their national office.

Home-Start UK,
2 Salisbury Rd,
Leicester,
LE1 7QR.
Tel: 0116 233 9955

Home-Start schemes help parents of children under five who feel under pressure. They offer befriending and support for families in their own homes. Local Home-Start schemes are available across the country.

Issue (the National Fertility Association),
509 Aldridge Road,
Great Barr,
Birmingham,
B44 8NA.
Tel: 0121 344 4414

Issue provides help and support to people with fertility problems. Offers factsheets and articles on infertility, local contacts and counselling by phone.

Marriage Care,
Clitherowe House,
1 Blythe Road,
London,
W14 0NW.
Tel: 0171 371 1341

Marriage Care provides across-the-country counselling for marital and relationship problems. It also offers help with fertility awareness, and natural methods of family planning.

MIND (National Associatioan for Mental Health),
Granta House,
15–19 Broadway,
London,
E15 4BQ.
Tel: 0181 519 2122
Helpline: 0181 522 1728

MIND has 200 local centres offering help and support for anybody who has concerns about their own or others' mental health problems. Find your local centre in your local phone book.

National Association of Citizens' Advice Bureaux,
115–123 Pentonville Road,
London,
N1 9LZ.
Tel: 0171 833 2181

Citizens' Advice Bureaux offer free and confidential impartial advice on any subject. They have 1,400 bureaux across the UK. They supply information on subjects such as social security benefits, housing, family and personal matters, money advice and consumer complaints.

National Council for Divorced and Separated,
PO Box 519,
Leicester,
LE2 3ZE.
Tel: 0116 270 0595

This organization tries to support people who have been through a marriage ended in divorce or separation. There are 115 branches nationwide, offering counselling and social activities. You can also obtain advice from this organization by post.

National Debtline,
Birmingham Settlement,
318 Summer Lane,
Birmingham,
B19 3RL.
Tel: 0121 359 8501

Runs a free, independent and confidential phone helpline for people in debt. Also offers a self-help information pack to callers.

National Family Mediation,
9 Tavistock Place,
London,
WC1H 9SN.
Tel: 0171 383 5993

Mediation can be very helpful after a couple have separated. Problem issues, such as property division, can be discussed in an impartial atmosphere with trained mediators. Mediators can also help couples to decide how best to maintain contact with children. Local mediation centres are listed in phone books.

Parentline,
Endway House,
The Endway,
Hadleigh,

Essex,
SS7 2AN.
Tel: 01702 554782 (Admin.)
01702 59900 (Helpline)

Parentline provides support for parents under stress and has 26 groups for parents, and helplines and drop-in centres.

Relate, National,
Herbert Gray College,
Little Church St.,
Rugby,
CV21 3AP.
Tel: 01788 573241

Relate offers relationship counselling at all of its 126 country-wide centres. Most centres also have a psychosexual therapist, who is specially trained to help with sexual concerns. To obtain the number of your local centre, look under 'Counselling' in *Yellow Pages*.

National Relate also has a bookshop that specializes in books on self-help and counselling issues. It offers a mail order service, and can supply booklists on various topics, including 'Marriage and Relationships', 'Sex and Sexual Prolems', 'Grief and Bereavement', 'Self Esteem', 'Stress and Depression', 'Sexual Abuse' and 'Divorce and Remarriage'. You can contact the bookshop on the number above.

SANE (the Mental Health Charity),
2nd Floor,
199–205 Old Marylebone Rd,
London,
NW1 5QP.
Tel: 0171 724 6520
London helpline: 0171 724 6520
Out of London helpline: 0345 6788000

Saneline offers information on all forms of mental illness, and offers support through its helplines and other care.